PUTTING AMERICA BACK TO WORK:

WHAT STATES & CITIES CAN DO

By William Schweke and Lee Webb
1982

Conference on Alternaive
State and Local Policies
2000 Florida Ave., NW
Washington, DC 20009
(202) 387-6030

The Conference is a national clearinghouse and policy research center for state and local officials and community leaders. In addidtion to providing research, analysis, and technical assistance, the Conference organizes frequent national and regional conferences and operates a nationally recognized publications program featuring innovative policy studies and legislative proposals.

ISBN 0-89788-070-6

PRINTED BY UNION PRINTERS

Table of Contents

INTRODUCTION

PUTTING AMERICA BACK TO WORK: WHAT STATES AND CITIES CAN DO

Unemployment in America is higher now than at any time since the Great Depression. Ten million men and women are out of work, and millions more go to work each day expecting it to be their last. American's dreams of their own home, a college education for their children, and a comfortable and enjoyable retirement are the enduring victims of the high unemployment rates.

For over two years the Reagan Administration has ignored America's rising unemployment. Arguing first that massive tax cuts would end unemployment, and more recently that lower unemployment was just around the corner, the Reagan Administration remains convinced that the federal government can do, and should do, nothing directly to put the unemployed back to work.

No major changes in philosophy are likely in the remainder of President Reagan's term. The conservative strength in both the House of Representatives and the Senate will stop Congress from adopting effective programs to get people back to work. Thus, in the midst of America's most serious unemployment crisis in decades, the federal government will not act.

America's state, county, and city governments find themselves, as a consequence, in a new and unique role. On the one hand, their powers and resources to do something about unemployment are far less than those of the federal government, yet in many cases their governors, their state legislatures, their mayors, and their city council members are more willing than President Reagan to act, and to act to the full extent of their powers and their resources.

The rising interest by state and local governments in ways to cut unemployment and create jobs occurs at the same time that states' powers and responsibilities are increasing in other areas as well. President Reagan's New Federalism is dramatically increasing the role of the state in the American government system. Many important federal programs have been abandoned, and decision-making authority for many others is being moved to the states.

What can states and cities do to create jobs? Conservatives and corporations argue at the state level for the same type of discredited strategy that Ronald Reagan has put into place nationally. They argue that a state can only increase jobs by improving its "business climate" through a combination of cutting taxes on corporations and the wealthy; granting additional property and income tax exemptions to new industry; weakening environmental and occupational health and safety protection; and rolling back unemployment and worker's compensation benefits. These Reaganite "solutions" have in fact been the most common state and local government response to job creation in recent decades.

However, new progressive ideas and programs have been crafted in recent years for state action toward full employment. In many states, such ideas have been translated into law, while in other states the ideas remain proposed legislation. More and more progressive state legislators, governors, local officials, trade unionists, and citizen groups are organizing to push for new legislation that, taken together, composes a progressive state program toward full employment.

This book, Putting America Back to Work: What States and Cities Can Do, was written to document and publicize these exciting new ideas. It is both a testimony to the creativity of progressive public officials and citizens in our states and cities, as well as a handbook for what our states and cities should do in the 1980's.

Putting America Back to Work: What States and Cities Can Do is divided into four chapters. The first, "State Strategies to Create Jobs," outlines a variety of possible state initiatives including the investment of public pension fund assets, stronger regulation of banks and insurance company investments and new state-financed venture capital corporations.

The second chapter, "Insuring Access to Employment for the Disadvantaged," details what a state or local government should do to insure that the poor minorities, women and young people get their fair share of jobs. Innovative uses of training programs and equal opportunity laws in various states and cities are outlined and described.

The third chapter, "Assisting the Unemployed," details what state and local governments can do to help the existing unemployed with their basic needs, and thus help them survive a potentially destructive experience. Areas of state action described in this section include improvements in unemployment compensation, pre-notification of plant closings to workers and communities, assistance in employee buyouts, and special assistance to low income workers.

The final chapter, "Protecting the Rights of the Employed," focuses on protecting workers from on-the-job problems that could cause them to be unemployed. Possible state initiatives, such as stronger workers' compensation laws, right-to-know legislation, and expanded protection for collective bargaining, are outlined in detail.

Each chapter begins with a narrative describing the overall program and range of possible policy initiatives. Next comes a description of existing programs and proposed legislation from a wide variety of states and cities. The final part is a detailed list of organizations, books, and articles the reader can turn to for detailed information about the general problem and about the innovative programs that are described.

As we enter the 1980's, high unemployment rates and a stagnating economy have made nearly all Americans fearful of the future. The failure of the federal government to face squarely the crisis of unemployment has forced many to look toward the state and local governments for ideas and for dramatic action. Hopefully, state and local governments will rise to the challenge of the times and will act agressively to help the unemployed and create jobs. Many of these new state and local programs may well become "models" for Congress in establishing new national programs when the political climate and leadership in America change.

Funding for this publication was provided by the National Council of Churches and the National Committee for Full Employment. Editorial assistance was provided by George Ogle of the United Methodist Church, Susan Phillips of the Industrial Union Department of the AFL-CIO and Woodrow Ginsberg of the Center for Community Change. And special thanks to Doug Bryant of the Health and Welfare Working Group of the National Council of Churches and Ellen Vollinger of the National Committee for Full Employment for their support.

William Schweke
Lee Webb

CHAPTER ONE:

STATE STRATEGIES TO CREATE JOBS

One of the most important issues that faces community groups and trade unions is how to create more jobs. Current high interest rates, high unemployment, and declining industrial production make job creation a critical problem that needs to be addressed in the 1980s. What can be done to create jobs and, specifically, what states and cities can do to create jobs, is the focus of this chapter.

In the past, full employment advocates have pushed, demanded, argued, and lobbied Congress and the White House for full employment, recognizing that the problem of full employment demands the resources of the federal government. While the need to maintain pressure on Congress and the White House is clear, it is important that state and local governments be encouraged to play a strong role in developing a full employment economy in the 1980s. The Reagan Administration's strong commitment to cutting back or eliminating federal programs that create jobs and assist the unemployed makes action by state and local governments even more urgent.

The following sections describe some of the innovative legislation that progressive public officials and coalitions either have succeeded in getting enacted or are fighting for. The three sections of this chapter are: (1) Enacting State Full Employment Planning Legislation; (2) Creating Private Sector Jobs; and (3) Creating Public Sector Jobs.

ENACTING STATE FULL EMPLOYMENT PLANNING LEGISLATION

One strategy for addressing job creation on a systematic and sustained basis is to enact state full employment planning legislation. This legislation can focus a state's resources on the goal of full employment and give employment advocates an excellent "handle" to build support for that goal.

An example of this kind of legislation is the Michigan Full Employment Planning Act of 1978. The legislation was drafted originally by the State Department of Labor, and was supported by organized labor. The act establishes full employment as a state priority and provides for the formulation of an employment plan. It has both advantages and disadvantages for activists.

The act does not set a specific employment goal, but instead defines "full employment" as "the highest level of employment which would provide an employment opportunity for every person able and willing to work, which is consistent with other public needs, and which can be attained during a given period of time by maximizing the investment of public resources toward that end."

An Interdepartmental Committee for Employment Policy is charged with developing a yearly employment plan, recommending policy, and generating up-to-date employment data. This committee is composed of directors of the major state executive and legislative departments.

In January of each year, the Governor and committee are required to submit to the State Legislature a final report that outlines a full employment strategy for Michigan. The report must assess the status of the recommendations of the previous year's plan. It must analyze economic and employment forecasts on a five year basis, evaluate the current state of the Michigan economy, and examine the state labor force. Lastly, the plan must propose programs, policies and reforms which will require either legislative or executive action. Hearings are supposed to be held by the House and Senate Labor and Commerce Committees to review the employment plan. Last year, however, the hearings were delayed for six months.

The Michigan Act has two principal shortcomings. First, it does not establish any structure for citizen participation in formulating the state full employment plan. Second, it does not provide for a period of public comment on the proposed plan.

This structure allows the Governor to dominate the planning process and to use the plan solely as his or her instrument. And, in fact, the Governor has used the planning process to campaign for his own conservative agenda of reducing government employment, reducing unemployment benefits, and decreasing business taxes.

The Michigan experience suggests that this kind of state law should be supplemented by additional public participation mechanisms. Furthermore, these citizen participation "levers" must be pulled by well organized and politically active groups in order to serve the needs of the unemployed, rather than conservative business interests.

CREATING PRIVATE SECTOR JOBS

The actual creation of new jobs is another issue that full employment activists must address. Employment opportunities can be created by either the private or public sectors.

Even among those who believe that government should be the "employer of last resort," most would agree that jobs in the private sector should be expanded as much as possible. This is reinforced by the fact that four out of every five jobs created are in the private sector. There are a number of strategies which can be pursued at the state and local level to improve the business climate and increase the opportunities for job creation in the private sector. Sometimes the approach used is to create conditions favorable to business, but unfavorable to workers. Such an approach obviously is unacceptable to those concerned with full employment. However, there are alternative strategies.

A critical factor in generating new and permanent jobs in the private sector is the investment of capital -- in the right amount and right form. Existing financial institutions -- banks, insurance companies, venture capitalists, investment bankers, and others -- appear to work reasonably well for large, established corporations, but increasing evidence indicates that appropriate amounts and kinds of capital are not available to all types of businesses. Among those enterprises which are disadvantaged in obtaining the capital they require, are small businesses (particularly new and young ones), enterprises located in depressed communities, firms in new business sectors, minority and women-owned businesses, and enterprises with nontraditional management and ownership structures: cooperatives, worker-owned businessses, nonprofits, and community development corporations. Since the largest number of new jobs is created in small business enterprises, this becomes a critical matter.

State governments have powerful leverage over private financial institutions. States regulate commercial banks, insurance companies, public pension funds, and other sources of business finance. Furthermore, state governments are also directly involved in capital markets with their loans, loan guarantees, revenue bonding, equity financing, and tax incentives.

Unfortunately, many of these programs do not effectively assist the kinds of business enterprises that are shortchanged by private financial institutions. In addition, certain traditional state programs like corporate tax abatements are ineffective in creating new jobs. Yet, state governments can play a more positive role, and can make financial institutions work more efficiently and more equitably.

Redirecting Public Pension Fund Investments

An important source of new capital for job creation is public employee pension funds. Redirecting these monies into small business, affordable housing, renewable energy development, and in-state corporations is a a strategy that offers a great deal of promise.

Why should employment activists attempt to redirect the investments of state and local public pension funds? First, state and local pension funds constitute an enormous pool of capital -- over $200 billion --and are growing at a rate of over ten percent per year. Thus, even a small redirection of assets into alternative investments offers tremendous possibilities for creating jobs and revitalizing communities. Second, public pension funds are structurally the most accessible to public accountability of all large financial institutions. Therefore, a campaign focused on pension funds has some natural advantages over ones aimed at other sources of business finance. Third, since the average return on public pension investments has been extremely poor (far worse than a passbook savings account), new alternative investments may improve investment performance.

And the job-generating potential of redirected public employee assets are enormous. For example, a computer simulation of the Wisconsin economy indicated that investing $20 million more in Wisconsin manufacturing enterprises would generate directly approximately 700 new jobs, $10 million in increased wages, 1,000 additional non-agricultural jobs, and $2 million in additional state and local tax revenues. Similarly, a California study of the employment, income, and tax revenue stimulated by $100 million of new housing investment by pension funds suggested the following: 1,840 construction jobs, 4,900 non-construction jobs, $144 million in increased income, $2.3 million in local taxes, and $16.6 million in state revenues.

To be successful, full employment activists must carefully craft investment proposals and management reforms to stimulate economic development and job creation, build political support, and neutralize one's opposition. One way to launch this long process of program development and political change is by creating a public investment task force, under the sponsorship of state or local government.

Such a broad-based, government-sponsored effort can develop the technical know-how required to conduct a careful examination of pension fund performance, needs, and alternatives. It can present additional opportunities for organizing, and it will bring the diverse pension fund actors together in one group for dialogue and decision-making.

However, it should be noted that creating a public investment task force is, in many ways, analogous to enacting a state full employment planning act. It is process-oriented and will be only as good as the governor or mayor who create it, the task force members who compose it, the staff who serve it, and the outside organizations who put pressure on it.

A good example of such an effort is in California. In 1980, under pressure from neighborhood organizations, progressive legislators, anti-apartheid activists, and the Campaign for Economic Democracy, Governor Jerry Brown established the California Public Investment Task Force to investigate the existing investment goals and performance of the state retirement funds and to recommend alternative investments. The task force is composed of trade unionists, retirees, business representatives, members of the financial community, policy analysts, and citizens. It has released an Interim Report and now is finishing its final proposals.

Initial recommendations included establishing a state industrial mortgage insurance program to stimulate small business financing, growth, and job creation. Both public and private pension funds would purchase a new mortgage-backed security created by the program. Investments in California venture capital, small corporations, and unlisted stocks were proposed as well. The report also suggested new investment initiatives for making housing more affordable and for stimulating construction jobs, including a preferential mortgage policy for employees and an interesting rental housing construction project. Lastly, the report proposed that the state pension portfolio be managed with a "conscience" and avoid investing in corporations causing social injury.

These investments would stimulate job creation in construction, solar energy and energy conservation firms, and high technology fields like communications equipment, engineering, electronic components, radio and television equipment, engineering and scientific equipment, medical instruments, and photographic equipment. Although it is impossible to calculate precisely how many jobs would be generated by new pension investment policies, one can make some estimates of their impact. For instance, if the pension trustees who control California's $30 billion in public pensions choose to use the proposed maximum 5% provision for investment in small- and medium-sized firms, nearly $1.5 billion could be made available. If they choose to use the 1% venture capital authorization, a potential $300 million could be made available for the stimulation of new industry. The latter investment could mean the creation of upwards of 15,000 new direct, indirect, and induced jobs in the state of California.

Since the formation of the task force, a Pension Investment Clearinghouse has been created with a $400,000 state appropriation. This new state office will collect and disseminate information on new investment oportunities, develop new investment vehicles, make policy recommendations, draft legislation, design demonstration projects, provide technical assistance to private and public funds, and set up regular meetings of pension managers to exchange ideas and develop and coordinate new investment strategies. Thus, creating a clearinghouse is a logical next step for pension activists: it further increases the technical capacity of funds to develop and manage alternative investments, as well as institutionalizes a forum for all the critical pension investment actors.

But if pension funds are to be increasingly placed in more employment-productive investments, it is not enough to simply establish a new investment decision-making process. Legislative changes in what a public pension fund can legally invest in also may be required. In fact, the pension fund investments which would do the most to stimulate economic development, employment creation, and new business formation are presently illegal in some state and local jurisdictions.

There are two recent legislative initiatives which employment advocates could undertake. In 1981 New York Program Bill 168 was introduced to rewrite the legal investment standards and goals of the state pension funds. These new provisions would allow investments in profitable small business and affordable housing construction and rehabilitation which were previously prohibited.

In 1979, the Massachusetts legislature passed a bill (S.1128) sponsored by State Senator Jack Backman which established a preference for in-state investments which do not sacrifice investment performance. Since then, the state pension fund has invested money for the first time in in-state Small Business Administration loans, as well as placed $19 million in Massachusetts residential mortgages last year.

Similar measures have been enacted in Minnesota, North Dakota, Ohio, Alabama, and a number of other states. This reform constitutes a critical plank in any pension reform agenda, which is encouraging pension boards and investment managers to seek out prudent developmental investments within the state.

If they are to be effective, employment advocates must win also the support of public employees and their unions. There are two state bills that illustrate two promising, but different, strategies to do this.

First, a new investment plan for pension funds could also include affordable financing for public employees (i.e., fixed and variable rate instruments, graduated payment terms, shared equity arrangements, low down payments, below market interest rates, et cetera.) California, for example is starting a preferential employee mortgage program which eliminates real estate closing costs, allows buyers a lower down-payment and offers fixed-rate mortgage financing. The program was created by the passage of Assemblyman Dave Elder's bill No. 1342. It is designed to stimulate jobs in the construction industry and make mortgage financing more affordable. Moreover, it constitutes an effective way to build employee and union support for innovative investments.

Second, public employees are anxious about the fiscal soundness of their retirement funds. Activists could address this problem by innovatively linking this issue with the jobs agenda. For instance, in Illinois, Representative Alan Greiman has authored and introduced legislation in 1981 which would link the state financing of unfunded pension liabilities with the issue of alternative investments. House Bill 0010 would amend the Illinois Pension Code and the Illinois Industrial Development Act. The bill provides for decreasing the unfunded liabilities of the state-funded retirement systems and financing a Special Economic Opportunity Fund to provide funds for investments which serve the need for industrial development, for small business creation and expansion, for the financing of owner-occupied residential property, for the provision of housing for senior citizens, and for neighborhood development.

The Illinois program allegedly would help to accomplish the following aims: provide an additional pool of capital for Illinois businesses and increase the industrial and job base in the state, assure that Illinois public pension money is used for the benefit of the citizens of the state, provide a long term program of partial funding of the unfunded public pension liability, and retard the departure of businesses from the North and Midwest to the sunbelt states.

Thus, mounting a successful job creation campaign using public pension funds requires effectively accomplishing the following actions. First, employment activists and their allies must formulate an overall strategy of job-creating investing that takes into account the particular employment and economic problems of their areas. Second, the campaign must establish by legislation a public pension investment broker, like California's clearinghouse, that can advocate for more innovative investments and can help to structure specific investment options for retirement funds in their state or their locality. Third, certain legislative changes in pension investment law must be enacted. These would eliminate archaic restrictions that impede prudent economic development investments. Other reforms would insure that employees were protected from unprofessional and corrupt investment practices, while still requiring reasonable efforts toward pursuing new job creating investments. Finally, a special political effort must be made to capture the support of public employees and other constituencies.

Financing Job Creation Through Enterprise Development

Because new products and technologies are critical to creating new jobs, new enterprise development is another issue that employment activists have to consider. Central to this new approach is meeting some of the financial difficulties experienced by new and young enterprises. The financing needs of start-up firms generally are not addressed by conventional financing institutions. Instead, seed money for these businesses often comes from personal savings, or loans from friends, family, and associates. Such investment gaps can cause the economic health of the entire economy to suffer -- new employment is not created, technologies are not developed, and higher returns of new and profitable enterprise development are not realized.

One method of addressing these problems directly is to create publicly chartered new product and venture capital corporations. To date, a number of state governments have taken this step. Full employment advocates attempting to create public financial institutions first must convince policymakers that such development finance corporations can fill financial gaps and can be operated in an efficient and nonbureaucratic fashion. Second, they must seek small business and other political support for their proposals. Third, they must design proposals to fit the specific comparative advantages and needs of their state: solar, high technology, and so forth. For example, a state heavily dependent on outside energy imports might want to develop a renewable energy sector. Likewise, an agricultural state could consider encouraging the development of a food processing industry.

Employment activists who live in states with a high-technology industry, for instance, might explore creating a state-sponsored venture capital corporation for financing new product start-ups. One example of such a development finance institution is the Connecticut Product Development Corporation (CPDC). This public corporation was established in 1972 to stimulate new technology development and job creation by providing risk capital to in-state enterprises which cannot obtain private financing. Its aim is to bridge the financial gap between product innovation and production, as well as product manufacture and sales.

In most of its ventures, CPDC supplies only 60 percent of the development costs and the private company incurs the rest. CPDC provides a grant of funds and, in return, receives a four to five percent royalty payment on sales. Thus, if a firm is not profitable, the Connecticut Product Development Corporation absorbs a loss. But if the venture is a success, CPDC stands to make a substantial return on its investment. Additional terms of its investment agreement require that the benefits of increased employment and tax revenues remain in the state.

The Connecticut Product Development Corporation is required to expend capital only for the costs associated with developing and commercializing specific inventions and products, not for operating expenses, basic research and equipment, land, or building acquisition or construction. CPDC also attempts to involve private lenders in financing these other costs and uses its capital investment to entice private commitments of money.

By the close of 1980, CPDC had invested $3.5 million in 36 businesses. Most companies that received funds are relatively small manufacturing or electronics firms. Original employment projections estimated that at the end of ten years of operation, 3,400 jobs for Connecticut residents would result, both directly and indirectly, from CPDC's efforts. Due to constitutional challenges and a slower rate of expeniture of funds than originally expected, it will take CPDC a little longer to reach these ambitious goals. But given its progress to date, it appears that this experiment is applicable to many states and large cities and is a promising vehicle for encouraging new product development, increased state economic activity, and permanent job creation.

Another source of financing for enterprise development is the life insurance industry. This model would tap the expertise of the private sector and use state fiscal and chartering powers to institute a new investment vehicle for putting more capital in in-state corporations and job development. The only example for such an an approach is in the state of Massachusetts.

Legislation creating a Massachusetts Capital Resource Corporation (MCRC) required the domestic insurance companies to capitalize a new $100 million investment fund, to invest capital in projects that meet the terms of the legislation, and to create a certain number of jobs per dollar invested in order to receive a tax break. For every qualified MCRC investment they make, the effective tax rate on these companies gets progressively lower.

Since 1977, MCRC has invested $35,412,938 in 36 businesses located throughout the state. Twenty-eight of the investments, totaling $20 million have been to small businesses. MCRC has calculated that their investment activities thus far have resulted in the direct creation or maintenance of over 4,562 Massachusetts jobs.

MCRC is an excellent model of how a state can encourage increased private sector investment through a combination of state financial chartering authority and a performance-oriented tax incentive. These two measures together can give the private sector enough of a push to marshall its enormous expertise and huge capital resources to create more in-state employment.

Full employment organizations in states undergoing rapid development of nonrenewable resources (i.e., coal, oil-shale, uranium, natural gas and oil, etc.) must address a different set of job creation and business finance problems. Their state governments and economies must prepare for the day when these resources are depleted. One solution is to tax the development of these minerals and fuels. Revenues from these taxes could be used to create a Trust Fund which would serve two purposes: (1) to finance the social, economic, and environmental costs that resource development imposes on rural communities; and (2) to finance the creation of public corporations that would invest capital in the diversification of the state economy away from being overly dependent on resource extraction.

One model of this type of development finance corporation is the Alaska Renewable Resources Corporation (ARRC), which was created by the state legislature in 1978 and funded in 1979. In its first year, ARRC financed 33 businesses with $20 million. Over 1,000 new jobs were directly created by these investments.

ARRC is the largest state-capitalized development bank in the United States and receives revenues in yearly intervals from the state's oil and gas royalty receipts. Its goal is to create an economy based more upon renewable resource industries. The Corporation allocates high risk equity and debt capital to private businesses owned by Alaskan residents in the fishing, forest products, energy, and agriculture industries.

ARRC is managed by a board of three full-time trustees appointed by the Governor. It can make equity investments for up to 49 percent of a company's outstanding stock and can make loans on any terms that accomodate the needs of a new or expanding business.

Yet, the ARRC also illustrates how politically vulnerable development finance programs can be. Some legislators felt that ARRC was not moving fast enough and did not finance enough ventures in their first year of operation. ARRC, on the other hand, argued that it had to operate as a prudent steward of state funds and could only finance businesses which showed promise. Moreover, there were not enough good deals in the state to move money at the speed that the legislature desired.

Eventually the critics of the ARRC won and the institution is presently not operating, pending a careful review of its operations. It is hoped, however, that it will start-up again soon after the evaluation is completed.

Still, the Alaska Renewable Resources Corporation is a promising model for states blessed with rich mineral resources. They could use a portion of their royalty incomes and severance tax revenues to capitalize a development bank for high risk entrepreneurial financing. ARRC also constitutes a model for predominantly rural states, which are relatively isolated from national business financing markets.

Another possible state strategy is to create jobs in the renewable energy sector. California, a leader in state renewable energy legislation, recently enacted a bill to create a State Assistance Fund for Energy, Business and Industrial Development Corporation (SAFE-BIDCO). The BIDCO loans money to solar businesses which are in the start-up phase or expanding their operations. It has a direct line of guarantee authority from the U.S. Small Business Administration which allows it to put a 90% guarantee on its loans and sell the guaranteed portion as a security in the secondary markets. Institutional investors such as pension funds and university endowment funds can buy these riskless securities, make a handsome profit, and enable the BIDCO to use the proceeds of these sales to make further loans. Such an arrangement allows the BIDCO to increase its funding base as much as 10 times its initial state capitalization of $2.5 million.

The SAFE-BIDCO is a development finance corporation well designed to specialize in financing particular types of technologies. It is structured so that it can take on more risk than a commercial bank. BIDCOs may also be helpful in mobilizing a new type of jobs coalition, including environmentalists, consumer organizations, appropriate technologists, solar industry lobbyists, and small businesses.

However, since a BIDCO is set up to work primarily with federal funding programs, many of the services it could offer could dry up due to recent and proposed budget cuts in federal loan guarantee programs. State governments could establish their own guarantee programs and increase the initial capitalization of the BIDCO. The BIDCO furthermore, could seek additional monies from conventional lenders. To the extent that they are effective in obtaining such monies, however, they would be constrained by the short-term nature of the capital and have to internalize the norms of conventional debt lenders, perhaps making the BIDCO both more passive in seeking deals and less willing to take risks.

The New York Job Development Authority (JDA) is another model to examine. JDA is a state agency which provides loans to in-state small businesses. Its bonding authority for making financing available was recently doubled to $300 million by a November vote of New York citizens.

JDA provides loans for financing fixed assets and real estate. No working capital loans or refinancing is available. Loan amounts are usually small, ranging from $20,000 to $30,000. The number of jobs retained or created and the location of the firm are two of the key criteria for loan approval.

Since its establishment in 1962, only two percent of the loans provided under the program have defaulted. Approximately 90,000 jobs have been created or maintained by JDA financing. However, despite this rosy picture, a recent IRS ruling 216 regarding bonding for state business finance programs may pose problems for JDA. The ruling may eliminate the floating of the type of tax-free bonds which are most helpful to financing small businesses.

The state of New York also is currently establishing a Rural Development Loan Fund, using monies from a U.S. Economic Development 304 Grant, a state cash match, and proceeds from two earlier business loans. These funds will capitalize a small rural development bank with $642,590 of capital, which can also be used to leverage additional private sector dollars. The loan fund is organized to create private sector employment and to expand economic opportunities for the unemployed and for low-income people, particularly in communities suffering from severe economic distress. All types of debt and royalty financing will be available and privately-, community-, and cooperatively-owned enterprises are all eligible for aid.

The Louisiana Small Business Equity Corporation (LASBEC) presently is being formed to stimulate the flow of private equity capital, to make long-term loans, and to offer additional financial aid to small enterprises in the state. It was created by 1980 legislation, has no funding yet, and will make direct investments, as well as make capital available to other in-state financial institutions: Small Business Investment Corporations (SBICs) Local Development Corporations (LDCs), Minority Enterprise Small Business Investment Corporations (MESBICs), and community development corporations.

In conclusion, full employment activists should note that most of the enterprise development corporations described in this section focused on creating jobs in economically dynamic high-tech sectors. Job creation encouraged by these institutions may help to tighten labor markets, but may not directly assist the hard-to-employ. Additional policy measures are required to effectively reach those on the bottom of the job pyramid and to deal with problems of skill upgrading, retraining, and declining industries and communities.

Getting Commercial Banks To Finance Economic Development

The American banking system is highly profitable, highly regulated, and insured to the point that bank failure is nearly impossible. Commercial banks devote most of their expertise and attention to financing big business and consumer debt, rather than small- and medium-sized enterprises and economically depressed rural and urban communities. Given the fact that commercial banks control over $1.7 trillion in assets, making this banking system more responsive to financing economic development and new job creation should interest employment advocates. Three ways to encourage banks to finance job creation are to pass legislation to establish a state loan loss reserve program, to create a linked deposits system, and to pressure state banking commissions to use their considerable power over bank lending practices.

A state loan loss reserve fund is a form of credit insurance. It could be established legislatively by either state or local governments. The fund would insure a negotiated percentage of the loan. The system would be financed equally by: the borrower, the lender, and the government. Each portion would be an actuarially determined percentage of the loan value based on the historical loss rates for this type of financing. Such a program would cost the government less than a guarantee program, adequately protect both borrower and lender, and increase the amount of moderately risky lending substantially. According to Derek Hansen's *Banking and Small Business*, the only such program ever enacted was in the state of California. However, this effort was never funded, due to the impact of Proposition 13.

In a linked deposits system, a state agrees to place its temporarily idle governmental dollars on deposit with a private financial institution. In exchange, the private bank agrees to make loans that fulfill publicly desired social and economic goals. Often, the state establishes a formal bidding process, in which private institutions bid for the funds and are evaluated by the government according to a formula which weighs interest paid by the institution along with their affirmative action procedures, lending practices to farmers and small business, and involvement in rural and urban development efforts.

Colorado, Illinois, Massachusetts, Indiana, and Missouri all have administered linked deposits programs. Indiana's program has been used to shore up a fledgling black-owned bank, while Missouri's has increased the flow of capital to in-state small enterprises.

In the past, linked deposits proposals have been pushed by coalitions of neighborhood groups, minority organizations, community-based development institutions, and other organizations concerned about the "red-lining" of communities by commercial banks and savings and loan associations. These groups, along with liberal local officials, are the strongest potential allies in any linked deposits campaign.

State policymakers, however, must be convinced that any loss of interest income will be made up in terms of increased jobs, more economic activity, and a stronger tax base. Another problem is that some recent analysis indicates state deposits may be too small to more than marginally influence private investment decisions. To overcome these doubts and concerns, organizers must develop a legislative proposal that builds upon the best features of existing models and that targets business lending practices, rather than housing mortgage lending practices.

Employment activists also should explore using state banking commissions to encourage job creation and economic development. State governments have enormous potential control over the lending practices of commercial banks.

A reform agenda in this area holds promise, although the organizing will be very tough. Banks, after all, possess, like pension funds and insurance companies, the capital to revitalize the nation's economy. Redirecting their practices could open up billions of dollars for new development programs with minimal government expense. Furthermore, it is conceivable that a well designed and argued bank reform platform could mobilize small business and some bipartisan support, as well as use entrepreneurial political vocabulary and rhetoric in its contentions. Yet, it will still be very difficult to enact, given the power of the banking industry, and its ability to play states off against each other.

One state, Massachusetts, already has taken action in this area. In 1979, Banking Commissioner Gerry Mulligan adopted as a directive to state banking regulators the language of the federal Community Reinvestment Act (CRA) regulations. Massachusetts CRA states that: (1) regulated financial institutions are required by law to demonstrate that their deposit facilities serve the convenience and needs of the communities in which they are chartered to do business; (2) the convenience and needs of communities include the need for credit services as well as deposit services; and (3) regulated financial institutions have continuing and affirmative obligations to help meet the credit needs of the local communities in which they are chartered.

Such a directive does not have the effect of a state law, but as long as the banking commission operates in terms of it, it is the equivalent. Later in the same year, the banking commission also required that all commercial banks to appoint a Community Reinvestment Act officer who would be in charge of compliance with state CRA directives.

Former California Deputy Banking Superintendent Derek Hansen argues that a state government could use these directives, as well as enact additional disclosure measures and commercial lending performance standards, to foster the involvement of commercial banks in community-based economic development. Banks then could be encouraged to set up additional investment vehicles such as Minority Small Business Investment Corporations (MESBICs), which would provide increased debt and equity capital for small firms in depressed areas. Likewise, banks could provide commercial lending staff in every one of their branches to ensure all communities more equal access to business financing.

An example of this approach is also in Massachusetts. Because of the pressure of these directives and a strong nonprofit advocacy organization, Massachusetts Urban Reinvestment Action Group, a Community Reinvestment Revolving Loan Fund (CRRLF) has been created. This $1.5 million fund is privately managed, but is financed by both an U.S. Economic Development Administration grant and $500,000 of loan monies from two prominent Boston banks, State Street Bank and Trust and the New England Merchants National Bank.

The overriding purpose of CRRLF is to target funds to three distressed areas in Boston -- Dorchester, Mattapan, and Hyde Park. In each of these communities, CRRLF will retain and create jobs for local residents, especially unemployed, low-income people. It will revitalize eight selected commercial strips and surrounding neighborhoods. Finally, the fund will attempt to increase the property tax base of the city and promote public investment in the infrastructure of these neighborhoods.

The administration of the CRRLF is primarily the responsibility of MURAG and its board of directors. The State Street Bank will train two MURAG employees in credit analysis and lend one of their bank officers for its first year of operation. The Merchants Bank will provide some marketing assistance. A Loan Administration Board of five community leaders will evaluate the appropriateness of each loan after each of the lenders have completed their analysis.

A full range of business financing options are to be available for borrowers and loan terms will be designed to meet the needs of the specific venture. Interest rates will range from four percent to the prevailing market rate and will usually be the result of a combination of part of the loan coming from one of the three participating banks, with the rest at low interest rates being provided by CRRLF. CRRLF is a model to watch, since it is a fascinating example of community, public, and private partnership in economic development.

In each of these new strategies, employment groups can attract support from those organizations, activists, and officials which have traditionally been involved in anti-redlining activities, housing organizing, etc. These coalitions are experienced in confronting and reforming bank practices. Full employment activists could learn from them and attempt to broaden their concerns to include the jobs issue.

Directing Capital to Depressed Areas

Employment advocates also should explore creating a state financial corporation which directs capital to depressed communities and the hard-to-employ. Presently, very few state financing institutions have an explicitly anti-poverty orientation that directs funds toward low-income areas. A financial program designed to address these problems would have three critical elements: (1) public capital must provide jobs with decent pay and benefits to those formerly trapped in poverty employment; (2) residents of economically depressed areas must have equal access to the physical capital put in place by state institutions; and (3) the enterprises created must offer job training, as well as entry-level jobs. Only one institution currently exists which includes these three components and targets its capital to disadvantaged local economies: the Massachusetts Community Development Finance Corporation. However, another version of this model has just been proposed in Wisconsin.

The Massachusetts Community Development Finance Corporation (MCDFC) is a concrete example of a publicly-capitalized venture capital corporation which makes investments only in businesses owned and operated by residents of the state's most economically depressed communities. Massachusetts CDFC acts as a development bank and provides both high risk equity and debt capital. The businesses in which CDFC invests must either be owned by or be in partnership with a communty development corporation (CDC), which is representative of the community. The Corporation's enabling legislation also requires that the ventures pay 1.5 times the minimum wage and have good fringe benefits.

Since its creation in 1976, Massachusetts CDFC has committed $2.8 million of its $10 million investment pool in 23 ventures. It has provided funds to 15 manufacturing firms, 6 retail/service businesses, and 2 housing/construction enterprises. Excluding the employment lost due to four bankruptcies and not counting the short-term construction jobs, approximately 265 jobs were directly generated by Massachusetts CDFC.

Despite its success in financing community-based economic development, Massachusetts CDFC has had to overcome a number of difficult obstacles. First, its start-up was delayed by a lengthy legal dispute over its constitutionality. Second, a technical assistance division, proposed originally, was eliminated from the version of the bill which passed. Consequently, CDFC had problems finding sound community-sponsored business and development ventures and was forced to radically slow down the rate at which it invested and lent its capital. (More recently, a Community Economic Development Assistance Corporation was created by state legislation and the organizational and managerial strengths of Massachusetts CDCs have been greatly increased by its activities. The Corporation provides a wide variety of technical assistance services including board training, legal services, market studies, and financial analysis.)

Wisconsin advocates have introduced somewhat similar legislation to create a Wisconsin Community Development Finance Corporation (WCDFC). The bill was enacted in March, 1982 and will create a nonprofit corporation for providing venture capital to business projects located in low-income communities.

The Wisconsin CDFC would be capitalized in the following manner. The state would appropriate state tax revenues for starting-up the corporation. Businesses or individuals could also purchase stock in the corporation or make charitable contributions to it. These investments would qualify for a 50 percent tax credit.

This combination of public revenues and private sector investments and donations would, in turn, be used to establish a Minority Enterprise Business Investment Corporation (MESBIC) which would draw upon $4 of federal Small Business Administration monies for every $1 invested. Thus, if the new Wisconsin CDFC is able to raise $1 million, its total investment authority would increase to $5 million. Of the two models described above, the

Massachusetts one is superior in terms of its financial structure (especially when complemented by a state-run technical assistance agency). The Massachusetts CDFC, for instance, does not have to depend upon corporate and individual donations and investments to be fully funded. It can, instead, draw upon the full faith and authority of state bonding powers to obtain the necessary capital. However, in states which are facing difficult revenue problems or which cannot legally float bonds to finance a development coporation, the Wisconsin model has much to recommend it.

CREATING PUBLIC SECTOR EMPLOYMENT

Public employment programs are necessary, if the hard-to-employ are to get jobs. Although the Reagan Administration has eliminated the public jobs components of the CETA program and has drastically cut back the U.S. Economic Development Administration, publicly sponsored employment still may be the most effective way to reach "high-risk" individuals whom private businesses will not employ, as well as address the social and economic problems that this country faces in the areas of housing, energy, health, education, and public works construction and rehabilitation. Putting the unemployed to work on community needs benefits everyone.

Given the fiscal constraints that states will face as a result of federal spending cuts, a convincing case must be made for scarce government funds to be spent for this purpose. There are, however four major areas where a powerful case can be made for using state revenues and bonding authority for creating such jobs: (1) investing capital in public works, (2) the retrofitting of state office buildings, (3) establishing a state conservation corps, and (4) creating a state counter-cyclical fund.

Generating Public Works Jobs

Public works employment offers some clear advantages to organizers. A very broad coalition can be built around using the unemployed to improve public facilities.

First, there is enormous work to be done. According to Pat Choate and Susan Walker's book, America In Ruins: Beyond The Public Works Pork Barrel, essential public facilities -- roads, bridges, sewers, wastewater treatment plants, et cetera -- are so deteriorated that the entire American economy may be threatened. For instance, half of the nation's communities cannot permit major expansion of existing firms or the location of new plants, because community wastewater and water treatment facilities are in danger of overloading. Furthermore, another quarter of our communities are hampered in job creation, because facilities such as roads, streets, and industrial waste disposal sites are either worn out, obsolete, or operating at maximum capacity. One of every five bridges requires major rehabilitation or total reconstruction, while the national interstate highway system has deteriorated to the point where almost one of every four miles requires replacement. Thus, a massive investment program must be undertaken if this critical infrastructure is to play a role in America's needed economic renewal.

Second, public works projects are good job generators. For example, according to the Council of State Planning Agency's report, Inflation and Unemployment: Surviving the 1980s, one billion in public works dollars would, initially and directly, create between 16,000 to 46,000 jobs (depending on the type of public works projectd). In addition, public works target effectively on the industries most affected by national recessions -- construction and durable goods. Third, such a program demonstrates "good business sense." Organizations who wish to improve a community's public facilities face a more certain, though no less rocky path, than do groups pursuing some of the other public jobs strategies described in this section. In fact, it is certainly easier to win a general community consensus for building roads and sewer facilities than for some other type of public employment program.

States, first, need to determine the nature and magnitude of public infrastructure problems to plan well-conceived public works projects that generate a substantial number of jobs, both directly and indirectly, and that provide the services necessary for private sector activity.

State governments should also explore financing alternatives. One way to finance this form of long-term investment in economic development is through the sale of municipal and state bonds. However, current market conditions present grave difficulties for state and local bond sales, difficulties which have been exacerbated further by the creation of the All Savers Certificate and recent efforts by the Reagan administration to diminish state bonding authority in the revenue bond area. Moreover, not all states have the power to float bonds. For instance, 13 states require a voter-approved referendum for the issuance of all debt, 12 states have imposed dollar limitations on the amount of debt that can be issued and require an approved referendum to exceed these limits, 6 states limit debt on a percentage of assessed valuation, 6 states limit debt on a percentage of state revenues, and 13 states limit debt only by an approved legislative authorization. Full employment advocates should examine carefully what restrictions may exist in their state and determine if these should be repealed in order to stimulate public works job creation.

Predominantly rural states could establish a bond bank. In 1969, the nation's first municipal bond bank was created in the state of Vermont. Since then, a number of states have followed suit. The Vermont Bond Bank is designed to help cure the credit and marketing problems its small cities face in issuing their own general obligation bonds. It packages a number of local bonds together into a single, larger offering sold under the bond bank's name. This action brings down transaction costs of the issue, gives the locality a higher bond rating than it could achieve on its own, and enables some very small communities to float bonds which could not otherwise do so.

Besides utilizing bonding authority, states can augment their capacity for financing additional public works by increasingly drawing upon user fees for sewers, roads, bridges, and utility hookups for new suburban housing developments. User fees, if applied selectively and in a progressive fashion, may reduce state tax expenitures, may avoid imposing an unnecessary tax burden on all state and local residents, may reduce the costs of public services over time, and may encourage city development, rather than suburban sprawl.

Retrofitting State Buildings

Many public buildings waste taxpayers' funds through inefficient and poorly managed energy systems. A rational investment in retrofitting these buildings could create employment for state citizens and conserve monies for other essential governmental programs.

Such a program should be very appealing to the public, particularly to those concerned about the prudent use of governmental dollars. In addition, those organizations and constituencies who stand to directly benefit from this investment of capital--small business, contractors, construction unions--can be mobilized behind the program. Moreover, employment advocates can convince public officials by pointing out a successful example in the state of Massachuetts.

In May, 1979 the state-wide citizens action group, Massachusetts Fair Share, proposed a massive program to weatherize all state government buildings. Mass Fair Share recommended that an $83 million state bond be sold in the tax exempt market to finance such an effort. Fair Share estimated that retrofitting government buildings would result in a 45 percent energy savings. The organization also calculated that the state would save $13.5 million in the first year of the program and $215 million over a ten-year period. Subtracting the total costs of the bond sale, this would result in a net savings of $80 million. Lastly, Mass Fair Share projected that thousands of new jobs in the energy industry would be created by this effort. For example, weatherizing 3000 state buildings would yield about 2400 man-years of direct employment and two to three times that number of indirect jobs.

Fair Share's proposal was converted into legislation and eventually passed as part of another bill, but with less funds than originally recommended. Since 1979, the state of Massachusetts has sold $42 million of state bonds to finance the retrofitting of state buildings and created an estimated 2200 jobs.

Establishing A State Conservation Corps

Employment activists, who wish to create increased youth employment should consider setting up a State Conservation Corps. The largest scale example of such a program is in California. It was created in 1976, under Governor's Brown's sponsorship, by Senate Bill 1575 and then reauthorized in 1980 by Senate Bill 1321.

The California Conservation Corps (CCC) is a model of an effective state program to create youth jobs. It undertakes projects that benefit the state and provide skills training for participants. Typical projects include developing parks, constructing coastal access, building trails, clearing streams, planting trees, restoring historical areas, protecting and improving wildlife habitats, and constructing access areas for the disabled. Approximately twenty percent of the Corps' time is spent fighting floods and forest fires.

The CCC includes over 1,200 young men and 600 young women. Each Corps member costs the state about $17,500. An independent consultant found that for every dollar invested in the CCC, taxpayers receive $1.20 in return benefits. Thus, the funds appropriated per year to support the program -- about $32 million -- have been an excellent investment of monies.

In addition, the Corps conducts literacy courses aimed at achieving a sixth grade compentency, provides some specialized job training, and is trying to improve its career placement and counselling services.

The California program also has been able to develop a strong bipartisan political coalition over the years. (Its reauthorization was voted in by 104 to 3.) In fact, a State Conservation Corps can probably be best sold by appealing to both conservative and liberal sentiments. Liberals can be won over by demonstrating the effectiveness of the program in renewing the environment, improving public facilities, and providing job training, education, and work experience for unemployed youth. Conservatives, on the other hand, can be sold with arguments about the role a Corps can play in decreasing youth crime and in building respect for hard work and discipline.

In addition to California's program, a few other states have sponsored youth conservation corps efforts. For example, in Florida Governor Bob Graham has appropriated $50,000 for designing a youth jobs program. The study is now being completed by the Department of Natural Resources and Florida State University. The Governor is expected to press next year for a $1.6 million conservation corps program. Pilot camps will be starting up in July and the entire program is to be administered by a nonprofit corporation.

Ohio is trying to keep its federally-funded Youth Conservation Corps program going with state funds. Previously, the program was financed with mostly federal funding. Because of national budget cuts, the state needs $7.1 million to continue it at its present level. A compromise bill was just passed by the state legislature and $3.6 million is to be appropriated.

Representative Mel King in Massachusetts introduced in 1981 a bill, HR 3020, to establish a youth employment effort. The legislation would create 50,000 public services jobs in state construction projects: low-cost housing, health care facilities, mass transit, day care centers, alternative energy development, recycling centers, et cetera. It would also set aside some funds for employing youth as paralegal and paramedical workers, social worker aides, lab technicians, artists, and musicians.

The program would include a job training component and would pay 1.5 times the minimum wage, or more if under collective bargaining agreements. Fringe benefits would include six months maternity leave. Additional attention would focused on employing the disadvantaged: women, minorities, disabled, individuals unemployed by plant closures, et cetera.

Not more than two percent of the funds would go into administration. Money would be raised by the following taxes: (1) raising the corporate profits tax to 6 percent, (2) imposing a 5 percent tax on professional services (i.e., architects, advertising, lawyers, etc.), and (3) instituting a 3 percent tax on the cash flow of real estate transactions above $100,000.

The program would be administered by state and local boards. The state board would be appointed by the Secretary for Manpower Affairs and would have representatives from civil rights, labor, youth, and womens' groups. Local boards would include representatives from minority and low-income communities.

The bill has been introduced for the past three years. Presently, it is "bottled-up" in committee. However, it is expected to be brought to the House floor this year.

Creating State Countercyclical Funds

State governments should explore creating state countercyclical funds to stimulate their economies during recessionary periods. Monies from such funds could be used for public works, public employment and training, and antirecessionary fiscal assistance. This would allow states to accumulate revenues during times of above average growth and spend additional dollars during periods of economic contraction.

The Michigan Budget and Stabilization Fund is the only example of such a program. It was enacted in 1977 to combat the state's tendency to have a drastic fluctuation in revenues, due to this dependence on the automobile industry which is strongly subject to economic cycles. The measure, which is often called Michigan's "rainy day fund," was an outcome of a bipartisan effort sponsored by Democratic Senator Kerry Kammer and supported by Republican Governor William Milliken.

Michigan's legislation allows a wide variety of uses of the fund: public works and public service jobs, refundable investment and employment tax credits for state businesses, and the stabilization of general revenues. The fund is triggerd by changes in real personal income and the state unemployment rate. At the end of FY'80 (September), the fund had accumulated $273 million. Approximately $265 million was withdrawn at that time and transferred into the general fund in order to balance the state budget. The remaining $8 million earned interest during the year, resulting in a total of $17 million. But since unemployment is still very high, all of this remaining money will probaly be directed into the general fund during this fiscal year.

Since the fund was started in 1977, it has not been used to finace any public works or public service jobs (due to the continued shortfall of tax revenues). However, in the first quarter of FY'79, there was a proposal to fund a prison construction project. However, this suggestion was rejected, because of fiscal constaints.

Thus, until now the fund has been a very useful fiscal tool to balance the budget. The state is now exploring ways to refine the triggering formula and is also seeking to build up the fund balance again in order to exceed past levels of accumulation. Economist Roger Vaughan of the Governors Office of New York has proposed to refine the Michigan model in his book for the Council of State Planning Agencies, Inflation and Unemployment: Surviving the 1980s. He argues that such state programs should replace federal discretionary countercyclical programs, which are ill-timed, ill-targeted, and not effective in creating jobs. Instead, each state should create their own anti-recessary funds, using state revenues, state and local borrowing during periods of low interest rates, local revenue contributions, and federal matching funds (approximately, $4 billion could be provided nationwide.)

This system would allow states to respond to economic cycles as they hit them and would not require them to wait for the U.S. Congress to act. It would also improve public works planning processes. Projects would be planned ahead and implemented when the state economy foundered. Monies could also be used to create new public sector jobs for the unemployed, as well as allow state and local governments to meet existing public service needs and maintain an adequate fiscal base.

SELECTED BIBLIOGRAPHY

Aronson, Leanne and Carol Schapiro. *The State's Role in Urban Economic Development*. Washington, D.C.: Urban Consortium Information Bulletin, Public Technology, Inc., September, 1980.

State economic development programs from an urban perspective.

Bearse, Peter (Ed.). *Mobilizing Capital for Economic Development: Institutional Innovation and the New Urban Policy*. Princeton: Center for New Jersey Affairs, 1978.

Excellent reader on development finance. Articles on resource trust funds and technology development corporations especially good.

Choate, Pat and Susan Walker. *America in Ruins: Beyond the Public Work Pork Barrel*. Washington, D.C.: Council of State Planning Agencies, 1981.

Analyzes the condition of public infrastructure in the United States and demonstrates the importance of public works jobs programs.

Coltman, Edward and Shelly Metzenbaum. *Investing in Ourselves: Public Pension Fund Investment Strategies*. Boston, Massachusetts Social and Economic Opportunity Council, 1979.

Outlines a detailed investment strategy for Massachusetts' public employee pension funds. Proposes and describes specific new investments, concentrating on the advantages and disadvantages of each.

Daniels, Belden and Michael Kieschnick. *A Policy Primer on Development Finance, Parts I-III*. Washington, D.C.: National Rural Center, 1979.

Superb primer on issues involving a progressive approach for business finance policies.

Faux, Jeff and Robert Lightfoot. *Capital and Community: Notes on Financing A New Economy*. Washington, D.C.: Exploratory Project on Economic Alternatives, 1976.

Describes how reforming the private financial system can lead to far-reaching economic change. Includes good basic information on existing innovative state programs.

Friedman, Robert and William Schweke (editors). *Expanding the Opportunity to Produce: Revitalizing the American Economy Through New Enterprise Development*. Washington, D.C.: Corporation for Enterprise Development, 1981.

A comprehensive reader which addresses the potential of, rationale for, barriers to, and means of increasing new enterprise development. Focuses particularly on how new and community enterprise development can be used to revitalize depressed areas.

Gordon, David. The Working Poor. Washington, D.C.: Council of State Planning Agencies, 1980.

Shows what can be done by a state to expand the economy's share of "good jobs." Reviews economic trends and examines quality of employment created by smaller businesses.

Hansen, Derek. Banking and Small Business. Washington, D.C.: Council of State Planning Agencies, 1981.

Provides a thorough review of private and public capital sources available to small business. Offers a wealth of specific and practical recommendations for improving bank regulations and fostering economic development.

Jacobs, Jerry. Bidding for Business: Corporate Auctions and the Fifty Disunited States. Washington, D.C.: Public Interest Research Group, 1980.

Criticizes business incentive programs. Documents their misuse by big business.

Kieschnick, Michael. Taxes and Growth. Washington, D.C. Council of State Planning Agencies, 1981.

Reviews and analyzes all empirical studies of tax incentive programs. Provides excellent material against conservative arguments.

Liebig, Michael. Social Investments and the Law. Washington, D.C.: Conference on Alternative State and Local Policies, 1980.

New legal study which extensively analyzes the meaning and often conflicting interpretations of pension law. Concludes that existing law can require pension trustees to consider social impacts of investment decisions.

Litvak, Lawrence. Pension Funds and Economic Renewal. Washington, D.C.: Council of State Planning Agencies, 1981.

Important study of pension fund investment strategies. Describes detailed and prudent investment options in areas of housing and small business.

Litvak, Lawrence and Belden Daniels. Innovations in Development Finance. Washington, D.C: Council of State Planning Agencies, 1979.

Explores the ways and means by which business capital is allocated, analyzes successes and failures of state business finance programs, and provides clear and progressive guidelines for state and local action.

Malone, Lawrence, and Robin Erdman. State Development Programs: A Catalogue. Washington, D.C.: National Council for Urban Economic Development, 1981.

Excellent overview of traditional state development programs.

McGuigan, Pat and Bob Schaeffer (editors). Developing the Public Economy: Models from Massachusetts. Cambridge, Massachusetts: Policy Training Center, 1979.

Includes articles on pension funds, bank regulation, plant closings legislation, innovative uses of CETA, and state tax incentive programs.

Nadeau, E.G. CETA and Private Sector Job Creation. Milwaukee, Wisconsin; Employment and Training Institute, Division of Urban Outreach, University of Wisconsin-Extension, June, 1980.

Contains thoroughly researched case studies of innovative community-based uses of CETA funds.

Nadeau, E.G. Creating Jobs Through CETA: A Proposed Economic Development Paper. Milwaukee, Wisconsin Department of Industry, Labor, and Human Relations, Employment and Training Services Division, October, 1980.

Recommends community-based economic development strategies as one of the best ways to link employment services with developing depressed local communities.

Nathan, Richard. Public Service Employment: A Field Evaluation. Washington, D.C.: Brookings Institution, 1981.

Evaluates favorably the experience of public service job creation in the CETA program.

National Governors Association. 1980-81 Policies for Community and Economic Development. Washington, D.C.: Committee on Community and Economic Development, 1981.

Outlines an agenda for state action.

Rifkin, Jeremy and Randy Barber. The North Shall Rise Again. Boston: Beacon Press, 1978.

Provocative study of role of pension funds. Describes a strategy to use retirement fund capital to structurally transform the U.S. economy.

Roberts, Benson, Robert Zdenek, and William Bivens. Community Development Corporations and State Development Policy: Potential for Partnership. Washington, DC: National Congress for Community Economic Development, 1980.

Includes excellent basic information on history and nature of community development corporations. Reviews state policies which could encourage their development.

Salisbury, Dallas (Ed.). Should Pension Assets be Managed for Social and Political Purposes? Washington, D.C.: Employee Retirement Benefits Institute, 1979.

Includes pro and con papers on the issues surrounding the social investment of public and private pension funds.

Schur, Robert and Marilyn Phelan. The Housing Crisis: A Strategy for Public Pension Funds. Washington, D.C.: Conference on Alternative State and Local Policies, 1981.

The best study to date on how to use public pension funds to make neighborhood-specific housing investments. Also, maps out a strategy for unions to become housing investors.

Schweke, William (editor). Plant Closings: Issues, Politics, and Legislation. Washington, D.C.: Conference on Alternative State and Local Policies, 1979.

Features specific, workable state and national policies that address the problem of plant closings.

Smith, David. The Public Balance Sheet. Washington, D.C.: Conference on Alternative State and Local Policies, 1979.

Proposes the use of a new concept to guide economic development strategies.

Sussman, Carl and Stephen Klein. Community Economic Development and the States. Washington, D.C.: Center for Community Economic Development, 1978.

Describes existing state programs which may be useful to community organizers and developers.

Sussman, Carl. The Massachusetts Community Development Finance Corporation: Legislation and Annotation. Cambridge: Center for Community Economic Development, 1979.

Comprehensive examination of Massachusetts CFDC legislation: history, purposes, and key features.

Vaughan, Roger J. Inflation and Employment: Surviving the 1980s. Washington, D.C.: Council of State Planning Agencies, 1981.

Describes and analyzes innovative new employment and anti-inflation programs for states. Includes excellent analysis of Michigan's "Rainy Day Fund."

Vaughan, Roger J. State Taxation and Economic Development. Washington, DC: Council of State Planning Agencies, 1979.

Demonstrates what's wrong with the present state and local tax structure. Outlines ways state and cities can improve the efficiency and equity of business and personal taxes.

Webb, Lee and William Schweke (editors). Public Employee Pension Funds: New Strategies For Investment. Washington, D.C.: Conference on Alternative State and Local Policies, 1979.

Primer on the issue of redirecting public pension fund investments.

CHAPTER TWO:

INSURING ACCESS TO EMPLOYMENT FOR THE DISADVANTAGED

Insuring equal access to job opportunities for the poor, minorities, women, and youth is a critical element of a full employment program. Presently, racial and sexual discrimination, poor education, age, residence in an economically disadvantaged community, and inadequate information about job openings all combine to make economic opportunities unequal.

Although federal governmental action is needed to overcome these barriers, states can help to address these problems in two ways. First, states administer federal- and state-financed employment training and placement programs which improve the skills of the unemployed and the poor and attempt to assist individuals in obtaining better-paying and more permanent employment. Second, state policymakers can promote equal opportunity by enacting and implementing fair employment statutes, by assisting disadvantaged workers, and by creating alternative work patterns for public employees. Employment advocates can launch organizing campaigns to strengthen existing programs and to implement new ones. The following sections of the chapter describe and analyze some existing state programs in each of these areas.

WORKING WITH STATE EMPLOYMENT PLACEMENT AND TRAINING PROGRAMS

State governments control the administration and delivery of a potentially comprehensive employment, training, and placement system. States administer critical parts of the Comprehensive Employment and Training Act (CETA) program, as well as run state-financed employee training programs outside the CETA system to fulfill the needs of private employers.

CETA is central to our national job training system. CETA originally was enacted in December 1973, marking a major decentralization of the policysetting, decisionmaking, and financial control of employment and training programs from the U.S. Department of Labor to state and local governments. The legislation was reauthorized in 1978 and expires on September 30, 1982.

CETA contains several legislative titles: Title II, A/B/C provides funds for job training and placement programs. Titles II-D and VI disburse public service employment funds but have been eliminated by the Reagan Adminstration. Title III provides a series of categorical programs for specific groups, including migrant and seasonal farmworkers, Native Americans, persons with limited English language skills, ex-offenders, and the handicapped. Resources for youth-oriented employment programs, including the Job Corps and summer youth employment efforts are funded by Title IV. Another youth jobs program -- the Young Adult Conservation Corps -- which was contained in Title VIII was also zeroed out by the Reagan Administration. Lastly, Title VII, the Private Sector Initiative Program is geared to induce business to hire the disadvantaged.

The agents for administering the CETA programs under Titles II, IV, VI, and VII are the states and those local governments that have been designated as "prime sponsors." Before a prime sponsor receives any CETA funds, the chief elected official must submit a detailed plan to the regional officer for employment and training of the Department of Labor. The "comprehensive employment and training plan" consists of a master plan and an annual plan. In formulating the comprehensive plan, a prime sponsor must consult with a planning council, which the prime sponsor appoints. The law also requires the council to include representatives of community-based organizations and persons eligible to participate in CETA programs.

Within this entire CETA program, states play a significant role. States control discretionary CETA grants to place individuals in existing jobs and help to create new ones. States serve as prime sponsors for rural communities, and control private industry councils in smaller, nonmetropolitan areas. Governors provide staffing and appoint representatives to State Employment and Training Councils which play a key policymaking role in coordinating employment service activities.

While the current employment and training system will likely undergo major changes when CETA comes up for reauthorization in 1982, the role which state governments play in the delivery of federal efforts will most likely continue to be significant and may even be augmented.

Using The State CETA System

The current state CETA system must be closely monitored to ensure that the programs genuinely assist the jobless and the poor. Although ultimate decisionmaking and spending authority now rests with the Governor, state executive departments, state prime sponsors, and private industry councils, advocacy and organizing by full employment organizations and coalitions can help to shape the programs offered, evaluate state government performance, administer portions of the programs themselves, and participate actively in the policymaking advisory councils.

There points of access are: (a) the Governors' Discretionary Grants; (b) the State Employment and Training Council; and (c) the Balance-of-State Prime Sponsors and Private Industry Councils

(a) Governors' Discretionary Grants

The Comprehensive Employment and Training Act (CETA) of 1973 required certain set-asides of funds at the state level that Governors can use at their discretion.

Four CETA set-aside programs currently exist: (1) the 1% Set-Aside for Educational Linkages; (2) the 6% Set-Aside for Supplemental Vocational Assistance; (3) the 5% Set-Aside for Special Statewide Youth Services; and (4) the 4% Set-Aside for Governors' Coordination and Special Services Plan.

The Educational Linkages grants can be used for encouraging coordination and establishing linkages between prime sponsors and education agencies and between prime sponsors and apprenticeship programs. In addition, the money also could be tapped for services jointly delivered by employment and training agencies and educational agencies and institutions. The Supplemental Vocational Education Assistance grants are used to encourage coordination between state-funded vocational education programs and the training activities of local prime sponsors within the state.

Of most interest to low-income advocates, minority organizations, and community-based organizations are the Governors' 4% grants and the youth services funds. Youth monies can be utilized to create statewide youth services including career guidance and counseling programs, apprenticeship projects in the building trades, employment training and work experience for ex-offenders, job search assistance, and interagency linkages between social and employment services within a state.

Governors' 4% monies can be used for employment and training systems development, technical assistance to local prime sponsors and state agencies, experimental programs and demonstration projects, research on collecting and using statewide labor market information, and special programs to assist specific target populations, such as ex-offenders or handicapped workers.

Funds may be spent directly by the state or given in grants to other agencies. State govenments also distribute 4% money through a competitive proposal process in which nonprofit organizations and public institutions propose innovative projects and seek funding.

Some states, notably Massachusetts, Florida, and California, have used 4% grants to encourage CETA-economic development coordination at both state and local levels. For instance, CETA training and job funds were allocated to the Florida State Association of Cooperatives, which is an association of county-level farming cooperatives assisting marginal black farmers to increase their incomes through cooperative training, supply, processing and marketing services. Massachusetts financed a State Business Information Center (BIC) Network with CETA dollars. BICs provide management and financial counseling assistance to existing and prospective small businesses through 24 local centers in the state. The East Los Angeles Community Union (TELACU) has also received CETA grants. TELACU administers a range of innovative job creation projects, including comprehensive training and placement services, a non-profit business used for training, and the development of a large industrial park.

(b) State Employment and Training Councils

Employment organizations wishing to affect the disbursement of state discretionary monies first must get information on who received aid in the past and what are the policy guidelines, eligibility criteria, and application processes for obtaining funds. Simultaneously, organizations must carefully examine existing and proven models of employment services, which seem to be appropriate for addressing state employment problems. Advocates may attempt to obtain a grant for a particular project, or may seek to influence the state disbursements of discretionary grants.

One method for changing the strategies of grant spending is to participate in State Employment and Training Councils. SETCs offer excellent organizing possibilities. The 1978 CETA amendments require the Governor to create a SETC and provide staff for it. The amendments also altered the composition of the Council and changed its duties.

Representation of local governments, which in operation translated into prime sponsors, was reduced from one-third to one-quarter. Percentages of representation were specified for the first time for other sectors. Such sectors include labor and industry, representatives of the eligible population and the general public, and representatives of service providers. In this last category, representation was expanded to cover the State Advisory Council on Vocational Education, the State's public assistance agency, and representatives of veterans organizations, and the handicapped. Furthermore, the new amendments specified that the chairperson of the Council be a public member.

Activists should get a list of the members of the SETC and determine if the chairperson is really a representative of the "public" and evaluate if labor, minority, women, and community-based organizations are adequately represented on the board. Full employment advocates should lobby for more representation of these types of organizations and constituencies on the council, as well as increase its efforts to build strong relationships with existing council members, which represent labor, community-based organizations, and CETA clients.

Thus, the SETC is a policy advisory body, to which Governors can turn in an effort to coordinate employment services in their states. Activists should designate it as an organizing target and pressure it to better serve the goal of full employment.

(c) Prime Sponsors and Private Industry Councils

The basic local unit which receives federal grants under CETA is called a prime sponsor. Prime sponsors can be states, local governments having populations of at least 100,000, or a consortium of local governments, one of which has a population of at least 100,000. Prime sponsors administer a wide variety of employment training programs, including classroom training, on-the-job training, work experience programs, skill upgrading, and retraining.

To receive its allocations of funds, each prime sponsor must establish three different advisory and planning councils. In addition, Governors must create and provide staffing for a State Employment and Training Council. (Some consolidation or variation of the current state and local prime sponsor advisory bodies is likely to be included in whatever system is authorized by Congress in 1982.) Currently, a local annual comprehensive plan must be reviewed by an advisory planning council, which is representative of the population eligible for CETA, including the unemployed, organized labor, community based organizations, the job service, vocational education agencies, and veterans' organizations.

This council has broad advisory responsibilities. It is assigned the task of helping plan the jurisdiction's CETA programs, monitoring and evaluating the performance of program operators, and providing continuing analyses of the need for employment and training services. Employment advocates should try to place their own members or representatives of allied organizations on these advisory councils or those which replace them.

In addition, currently a special youth council must review plans for Title IV youth programs; and a private industry council (PIC) must review and approve plans for any program funded under the Title VII Private Sector Initiative Program. Private Industry Councils (PICs) give the business community and economic developers a chance to design and operate CETA programs together. PICs attempt to increase private sector employment and training opportunities for eligible CETA participants.

Each Private Industry Council must have a majority of members who represent local private businesses. Membership also must include representatives from organized labor, community organizations, local education agencies, and local economic development agencies.

PICs have direct responsibility for programs funded under Title VII. Programs allowed under Title VII include classroom and on-the-job training, upgrading and retraining, work experience, skills assessment, and counseling and placement of clients -- everything authorized under other CETA titles except public service employment. PICs may establish special programs for youth or other disadvantaged groups. The emphasis in all Private Sector Initiative programs is on eventual placement in jobs in the private sector.

State governments, moreover, are responsible for services in areas too rural or too sparsely populated to be prime sponsors on their own. They, thus, establish prime sponsors and PICs for areas with populations of less than 100,000. These cities and counties are called "balance-of-state" areas. And in both cases, the CETA system operates much as it does in those communities that qualify as independent prime sponsors. For example, prime sponsor planning councils must be set up to advise prime sponsors.

So far, most PICs have simply funded ongoing programs begun by prime sponsors under other CETA titles. In fact, PICs' choice of programs often seems to parallel that of traditional CETA service planners and providers, although with more classroom training and on-the-job training, rather than work experience, skills assessment, and job counselling.

However, in Boston, the Massachusetts Community Economic Development Assistance Corporation (CEDAC), a quasi-independent state body providing technical assistance to community development corporations and other non-profit community-based organizations in economically depressed portions of the state, is working with the Boston Private Industry Council on a demonstration grant to explore new ways in which PIC employment and training programs can be integrated with community-based economic development activities. Funded in part by the National Alliance of Business, the program is specifically designed to develop a replicable project through which PICs and community-based organizations can work together.

The project, which began in June 1981, is examining existing cooperative relationships between local employment and training agencies and community development corporations nationwide to define the current state of the art and propose new collaborative strategies and relationships. As part of this effort, CEDAC also is developing an employment needs assessment handbook for use by community development corporations to better direct their job creation, placement, and training efforts, conducting a training program for both CDCs and prime sponsors and PIC personnel, aimed at fostering greater understanding of each other's activities and organizations, and implementing several projects with Boston CDCs to demonstrate and refine practical working relationships with local employment and training agencies.

Full employment organizations should closely follow the evolution of this project. Successful completion of its goals could suggest a number of new strategies for ensuring that PICs serve the interests of the jobless and the poor.

Once again, employment advocates should focus their organizing campaigns on the advisory councils attached to these institutions. In both programs, full employment advocates should meet with these councils, examine how representative existing members are, place allies or members of their own organization on these councils, and develop strong ties with the council members who represent their constituencies and who are sensitive to the needs of the unemployed.

Establishing Customized Employer Training Programs

One of the most common employment development programs currently administered by states are customized training programs. Millions of dollars are spent by state governments every year on training workers to meet the specific needs of an employer. These vocational programs have different names in different states -- in South Carolina, "Special Schools," in Minnesota, "New Jobs," and in Texas, "Profit-Train."

Unfortunately, most of these programs have problems. First, they not only provide state-subsidized job training at little or no cost to businesses wishing to expand or start-up in the state, but they also are used to "pirate" industry from other states. Second, they often train workers for low-paying and non-unionized jobs. Third, these programs are even sometimes used to screen workers for labor union background.

Thus, employment advocates who want to campaign for training programs that assure trainees of jobs and which are more attuned to the skill needs of area business may have to reform existing programs or develop new ones which are more sensitive to the interests of employees. Such programs should demonstrate more balance between job attitudes that benefit the individual and attitudes that benefit the employer, balance between the costs to the taxpayer for education and costs to the company for training, and balance between education for long-term career opportunities and education for short-term job opportunities. With these elements in mind, customized training programs can help to create new employment and assure the unemployed and the poor of greater economic opportunities.

An example of such a state-sponsored training program is the California Work Site Education and Training ct (CWSETA) which was enacted in 1979 to help individual employers meet their specific demands for trained workers. CWSETA is based on the idea that employers know best their own training needs and that employees learn best on the job. CWSETA requires employers to participate in both designing and operating a training effort. The program, in fact, borrows heavily from the experience of apprenticeship and some of its projects include formal apprenticeship instruction. But all projects typically include both classroom training, often after working hours, as well as employer-sponsored on-the-job training.

Almost 300 employers are now involved in the training of 6,000 persons. Initial programs have focused on training workers for the electronics and aerospace industries, machine trades, and nursing. In each area, California has been experiencing acute manpower shortages with employers recruiting from out of state to meet their needs. Other training programs have been created for automotive mechanics, restaurant chefs, farm workers, and drafters.

Projects have been established for both entry level jobs and for upgrading the skills of employees already working for the participating employers. Some efforts have provided career mobility for present workers and then filled the lower level slot with a person from the CETA system. CWSETA has even been tapped for retraining efforts aimed at victims of plant closings.

The California Employment Development Department presently administers a $25 million state appropriation to pay the extra costs incurred by employers and schools in providing training. The department also is required to monitor and assist on-going projects.

State Youth Job raining and Placement Programs

A number of states are initiating job training and placement programs aimed at youth. Delaware presently administers a program, which also is operating on a pilot basis in portions of Massachusetts, Arizona, Tennessee, and Missouri. The program, Jobs for America's Graduates, identifies young people still in school who are most likely to become unemployed, and provides them with basic employment seeking and keeping skills. Job opportunities in the private sector are located and graduates are placed and followed through for up to nine months. The program is run by a board of leaders, representing government, business, education, labor, and the community.

Another youth program is getting underway in Wisconsin. The Wisconsin Youth Initiative attempts to better coordinate the efforts of agencies and programs that educate and train in-school and out-of-school youth, ages 14-21. The program, first, comprehensively assesses each eligible youth, identifying weaknesses and deficiencies in his/her academic and employability skills. Second, it gives eligible youth the appropriate educational, social, and training services, as suggested by the assessment. Third, Wisconsin's program helps the local school systems develop programs to reduce drop-out and truancy problems through alternative schooling, work experience, career education, and expanded education in the public schools. Fourth, it expands basic skills education available and make it attractive to out-of-school youth. Lastly, Wisconsin Youth Initiative attempts to develop new private sector employment opportunities and engage business participation in the design of training programs.

All of these programs are delivered through a combination of institutions, including CETA prime sponsors, community-based organizations, the Job Service, and public schools. Funding is from both federal and state sources, including significant amounts of CETA and vocational education monies.

PROMOTING EQUAL OPPORTUNITY

Full employment is impossible without equal employment opportunity. Without it, many minorities and women will continue to be condemned to low-paying, unstable jobs, with limited possibility of advancement. The Federal Government of course, is the most important actor in trying to make equal opportunity a reality. But recent actions and appointments regarding Title VII enforcement threaten a federal retreat from our nation's commitment to equal rights.

During the next four years, progressive state and local governments may bear an additional burden in ensuring equal opportunity. A number of state policymakers already have begun to develop programs and policies to help meet this challenge by continuing to improve employment opportunities for minorities, women, youth, seniors, and the disabled.

Enacting and Implementing Fair Employment Statutes

Implementation of fair employment statutes by states could be a step toward preventing discrimination and ensuring that minorities, women, and the disadvantaged have an equal opportunity in employment hiring and recruitment, job assignments and career mobility, and employer training programs. In 1980, legislatures in 23 states addressed these problems by passing new laws and/or strengthening existing ones.

An Illinois law, which went into effect on July 1, 1980, covers "unlawful discrimination in employment, real property transactions, access to financial credit, and public accommodations." It authorizes the creation of a Human Rights Commission charged with adjudicating allegations of unlawful discrimination. In Alaska, prohibitions on employment discrimination in the private sector were extended to the state and its political subdivisions. In Kentucky, prohibition of wage discrimination based on sex now applies to employers of two or more persons, rather those having eight employees or more as before. In Michigan the fair employment practices law now will apply to all employers rather than those only having four or more workers. Connecticut and Michigan also passed legislation to prohibit sexual harassment.

In 1981, California established a policy of "comparable worth" in setting salaries in state government in jobs dominated by women, on the basis of the value of work performed. Resolutions also were passed in Hawaii urging all employers to adopt this concept of equal pay for work of comparable value.

Full employment advocates must work to ensure that state governments enforce the statutes in an aggressive fashion and design employer practices within the public sector which promote equal opportunity. Two effective strategies are: (1) creating a state legislative task force for evaluating state affirmative action practices, and (2) establishing a career ladder program for public employees.

In 1979, Pennsylvania House Resolution No.65 was introduced, but not enacted. It called for the creation of a special committee to monitor and investigate the affirmative action programs of state departments and agencies, including the activities of the State Civil Service Commission. In addition, it would evaluate governmental compliance with equal opportunity laws in the governmental purchase of services from businesses. Such a resolution would be a highly public way to examine the practices of state government in complying with federal law and state fair employment statutes.

Other efforts have been aimed at ensuring equal chance for advancement. Some states have enacted legislation which mandates the creation of upward mobility programs for public employees in low-paying occupations. Such possibilities for advancement are critically important for minorities and women, who hold the greatest percentage of these jobs at the bottom of the employment pyramid.

California Assembly Bill 3756, which was passed in 1977 and constitutes Article 4.5, California code 19400-19409, strengthened the implementation of state affirmative action plan by requiring all state departments to establish effective upward mobility programs. The programs will provide career and academic counseling and a range of training programs including college programs offered at the worksite with release time at reduced or no cost to the employee.

In 1976, the Connecticut legislature passed a bill which called for the formation of a committee to determine how career counseling and training opportunities can be made available to state employees. The implementation of the upward mobility program will establish specific annual goals on the number of entry level professional, managerial, and administrative positions that are to be available to part-time employees and to increase the number of permanent part-time positions available. Likewise, Maryland has enacted legislation which provides that one percent of the positions at each and all levels in every executive agency shall be filled by permanent part-time employees. An important feature of this law provides that employees shall be eligible, on a pro-rated basis, to receive benefits available to full-time employees.

Assisting Displaced Homemakers

Displaced homemaker legislation programs provide services and employment aid to help homemakers affected by dissolution of a marriage or other loss of family income. Such measures have been passed in thirty states.

This legislation establishes multipurpose centers which provide displaced homemakers with counseling, job training, and referral services to help them to secure employment. Some of the bills also seek to create new public sector jobs that meet identified needs in the community and which could be filled by displaced homemakers.

The enacted Colorado House Bill 1114 is a good example of this type of legislation. It creates a series of multipurpose service centers. Each service center is required to offer job counselling services "specifically designed for displaced homemakers." Job training and placement services also will be provided to either assist displaced homemakers in gaining admission to existing public and private job training programs and opportunities or attempt to develop new public and private training and placement programs. Centers can work to create new jobs for displaced homemakers in the public and private sectors to meet community needs. In addition, these centers can offer a wide range of other counseling services in the health education area, legal problems, alcohol and drug abuse counselling, and financial management.

The Displaced Homemaker Center in Alameda County, California has initiated some of the most innovative and creative job development strategies. By assessing community needs and focusing on expanding existing job opportunities for older women, they have developed a training program for women who are willing to pioneer new jobs. Consequently, the center has developed new jobs including marital dissolution counselor, widow-to-widow counselor, aging programs specialist, home health care technician, and nursing home ombudsman.

Most states have displaced homemaker legislative on the books, with the following exceptions: Alabama, Alaska, Georgia, Idaho, Indiana, Missouri, Mississippi, Pennsylvania, Tennessee, Utah, Vermont, Virginia, West Virginia, and Wyoming. In addition, activists should look into whether funds have been appropriated, or whether programs need to be strengthened.

Creating Alternative Work Patterns

Full employment advocates who are interested in spreading employment opportunities more widely, should examine the proposals for job restructuring which are surfacing in state legislatures and municipalities throughout the country. (Also, see discussion of short-time compensation in chapter four.)

A number of proposals for job restructuring have been proposed in state legislatures and municipalities throughout the country. Support for various programs of job restructuring has been increasing from both men and women workers who want to adjust their jobs to suit child care and other personal needs. Senior citizen groups have encouraged the development of such alternatives which meet the needs of older workers, or provide a transition to retirement.

Job sharing is one option for part-time or part-year work. It is a voluntary work arrangement in which two people both hold responsibility for what was formerly one full-time job. They divide salary, time on the job, and fringe benefits. This arrangement differs from permanent part-time employment, in that it allows for the creation of two part-time jobs where one full time job previously existed.

Madison, Wisconsin has had a small number of employees opt for job sharing arrangements under administrative guidelines for the city. Legislation in Oregon directs the Budget Management Division of the Executive Department to submit analysis of job-sharing in state agencies to the legislature. While in Colorado, Governor Lamm issued an Executive Order in 1978 urging state agencies to utilize the concept of job sharing.

Flexible hour scheduling -- where the employees set their own arrival and departure times -- has been used to accomodate workers who wish to adjust their working hours to accommodate child care responsibilities, education, and advanced training programs, and other personal needs. While flex-time systems vary, most establish a core time of about four hours mid-day when the employees must be on the job. Employees may start and finish work at their own discretion, as long as they work within a set time and complete the total of hours required per day.

California Assembly Bill 914 is a good model for programs for flexible working hours for public employess. It requires each state department to develop its own plan for flex-time employment with core hours and "band-width" hours which specify the earliest and latest time an employee may work. The bill declares that "flexible working hours would enable each employee to schedule individual working hours so as to avoid the traffic rush hours, or to provide free time for family leisure and personal business, thereby increasing morale and productivity among state employees."

Some state governments have expanded part-time employment opportunities. During the past five years there has been some legislative movement in this area. Some states have sought to improve the benefits available to part-time employees and to increase the number of permanent part-time positions available. For instance, Maryland has enacted legislation which provides that one percent of the postitions at each and all levels in every executive agency shall be filled by permanent part-time employees. An important feature of this law provides that employees shall be eligible, on a pro-rated basis, to receive benefits available to full-time employees.

However, there are some problems with the proposals. Some flex-time proposals eliminate the required hours per day and allow an employee to work ten hours one day and six the next. This concept conflicts with laws requiring overtime pay for more than an eight hour day, or extra pay and bonuses for working swing and night shifts. Also during periods of high unemployment, increased part-time work opportunities may lessen the number of full-time jobs. Many unions have expressed concern about these proposals undermining hard-won worker protection provisions, and are seeking ways to address these issues. These concerns must be genuinely addressed in the development of any campaign for an increase in part-time job opportunities.

SELECTED BIBLIOGRAPHY

Bernstein, Scott and James Pitts. Making CETA Work: For Workers, For Neighborhoods. Chicago: Community Renewal Society, June, 1979.

Contains useful information on how to run a CETA project aimed at stimulating community-based development.

Center for Community Change. A Citizens' Action Guide to CETA. Washington, D.C.: April, 1979.

Provides an excellent overview and analysis of the different titles of the 1978 CETA legislation.

Fischer, Jospeh. CETA and Economic Development Coordination: A Guide for Local Officials and Administrators. Washington, D.C.: National Council for Urban Economic Development, July, 1981.

Guide to CETA system and how it can be used to foster job creation and economic growth.

Ginzberg, Eli (editor). Employing the Unemployed. New York: Basic Books, 1980.

Excellent survey of programs, problems, and future of employment service and public jobs programs in the United States.

Grune, Joy Ann. Manual on Pay Equity: Raising Wages for Women's Work. Washington, D.C.: Conference on Alternative State and Local Policies, 1980.

Reviews "equal pay for work of comparable value" movement: legislative initiatives, litigation, news of organizing campaigns, studies, and collective bargaining agreements.

Kazis, Richard and Peter Sabonis. Leveraging With a Toothpick: The Carter Administration's Private Sector Strategy for Job Creation. Washington, D.C.: National Center for Jobs and Justice, September, 1979.

Early analysis of Private Industry Councils of CETA. Includes some organizing strategies.

Sekera, June. Meshing Economic Development With CETA: Model State Programs. Washington, D.C.: National Governors Association. April, 1981.

Contains a series of case studies of innovative CETA-economic development programs.

Vaughan, Roger J. Employment and Training: What's Wrong With the Present System and What Can Be Done About It. Washington, D.C.: Council of State Planning Agencies, July, 1981.

Discusses the importance of an effective employment and training policy. Focuses on the role of state and local governments as well as creative possibilities in the private sector.

W.E. Upjohn Institute for Employment Research. Work Sharing Case Studies. Kalamazoo, Michigan: 1981.

Assesses the experience of employers who have had a variety of work sharing arrangements including phase retirement, rotation layoffs, and shorter work weeks.

Work in America Institute. New Work Schedules for a Changing Society. Scarsdale, New York: 1981.

Concludes that flexible work schedules increase productivity through fewer absences, better use of facilities, and improved employee morale.

CHAPTER THREE:

ASSISTING THE UNEMPLOYED

Unemployment is likely to remain a major problem in the near future, with many people unemployed due to President Reagan's economic policies. Programs to assist the jobless must be an important part of the progressive organizing agenda.

The unemployment insurance program has been the mechanism through which a measure of protection has been provided to the unemployed. While hardly a panacea for the jobless, the program provides them with essential income, helping many American families to meet the bare necessities of life. Moreover, in times of high unemployment, the benefits program helps to keep consumer buying power effective. With layoffs increasing and the recession expected to deepen further, the program will be even more essential in the months ahead.

Unemployment insurance programs vary widely from state to state and possess a number of serious deficiencies which should be corrected at the federal level. However, recent federal initiatives have worsened, not corrected, the situation, as benefits and coverage have been drastically cut. In the current political climate, with positive national action unlikely, innovative state efforts are vital.

Employment activists can push state governments to play a stronger role in assisting the unemployed. Many elements of the unemployment insurance system -- including benefit levels and eligibility requirements -- are under state jurisdiction. States can assist victims of plant shutdowns by requiring advance notice of the closings, and by providing income maintenance, retraining, mobililty assistance and homeownership aid, and adequate health care insurance. Public officials and activists can better meet basic low-income needs by assisting those on welfare to obtain decent employment and by helping to provide access to hospital care for the needy and unemployed.

REFORMING UNEMPLOYMENT INSURANCE

Unemployment insurance is a worker's first line of defense against the hardship of unemployment. State governments control many of its most critical features. Employment advocates should examine the degree of protection that their state system provides the unemployed. A reform agenda might increase benefit levels; liberalize disqualification and eligibility requirements; ensure due process in disputes between claimants, the employer, and the state; create a short-time work sharing program; and modify unemployment compensation to encourage retraining and mobility.

Some changes will be much easier to enact than others. Employment activists should, therefore, carefully analyze the possible advantages and disadvantages of each possible reform while planning an organizing campaign.

Protecting the Jobless

The nation's system of unemployment insurance is a unique national and state partnership. It is based upon federal law, but executed through state law and administration. Unemployment insurance was created to provide adequate benefits to protect workers during temporary periods of joblessness. Benefits are payable as a matter of right to workers who have enough qualifying wages and yearly work experience to meet their state's minimum conditions, who are free from disqualification on the basis of their separation from their last place of employment, and who are ready, willing, and able to work.

Unemployment insurance was created by the Social Security Act and the Federal Unemployment Tax Act. These laws lay down the basic framework of the system. The Federal government prescribes minimum standards of coverage of workers, which states are to exceed. State unemployment insurance law, however, decides most of the substantive questions about particular unemployment insurance programs. For instance, state laws establish the minimum amount of work necessary to qualify for benefits, the weekly benefit amount, the number of weeks benefits are payable, the circumstances under which benefits may be denied, the length of such denial, the tax structure to fund the program, and the method of allocating benefit costs among employers. Consequently, laws vary greatly from state to state in the degree of protection and responsiveness which they provide to the unemployed.

a) Eligibility and Disqualifications

Employment advocates, first, could pressure states into providing fair disqualification requirements and liberal eligiblity conditions. For example, disqualification should not be allowed in cases of voluntary quitting for "good cause." Good causes may include sexual harassment and compelling family circumstances. State law also should provide that disqualifications, including voluntary quits, discharges due to misconduct, refusals of suitable work without good causes, and some types of labor disputes, be limited to a benefits postponement of from one to six weeks, rather than indefinite disqualification, as is the case in some states. Furthermore, the length of such disqualification should depend on the circumstances of the case. All disqualifications should end when the unemployed claimant accepts other work. In other words, disqualifications should not carry over into new periods of unemployment. (Illinois has such a statute.)

Employment advocates also could consider reforming state laws covering the issues of "misconduct," "labor dispute," and "suitable work" in a fashion sensitive to the worker's interest in maintaining an adequate income and encouraging an individual to improve his or her standard of living. The UAW recommends that "misconduct" should be of a gross nature and involve willful action by the worker. Moreover, the duration of the penalty, as noted above, should depend upon the degree of misbehavior.

Likewise, a "labor dispute" should not be grounds for complete disqualification. Benefits should be paid in particular circumstances. States should follow the lead of New York and Rhode Island, which allow unemployment benefits to be paid to strikers after a seven to eight-week waiting period.

Victims of lockouts also should be able to collect benefits. Sixteen states -- Arkansas, California, Colorado, Connecticut, Georgia, Kentucky, Maryland, Michigan, Minnesota, Mississippi, Ohio, Oklahoma, Pennsylvania, South Dakota, Utah, and West Virginia -- have this provision on their books. Nor should strikes due to unlawful employer conduct disqualify workers from receiving unemployment insurance. West Virginia has such a statute, covering strikes arising from an employer's resistance to collective bargaining.

b) Job Search

States should eliminate also specific "actively seeking work" availability requirements and instead should require job search efforts by the claimant that are appropriate in light of such relevant factors as the hiring practice of the claimant's industry, the local labor market, conditions of the worker's occupation, and the claimant's particular circumstances. The definition of suitable work also should include the issue of fringe benefits, as is the case in the states of Indiana and Michigan. For example, "suitable work" is employment that has wages, health insurance, and pension benefits comparable to an individual's previous job. Furthermore, individuals should continue to be eligible for benefits if they become temporarily ill or temporarily disabled after they have filed a claim, provided there is no suitable work offered to them and they are not receiving disability insurance payments for the same incapacity.

c) Waiting Week

States could also lift "waiting period restrictions." Most states do not allow benefits to be paid for the first week of an individual's unemployment that begins after a claim is first filed. This unjustly penalizes the unemployed individual, for whom such a benefit is often critical to meet basic needs. The waiting period should be lifted in states that have it. Twelve states -- Alabama, Connecticut, Delaware, Iowa, Kentucky, Maryland, Michigan, Nevada, New York, Virginia, and Wisconsin -- have no waiting period before benefits begin.)

Unfortunately, recent U.S. Department of Labor regulations have created a new obstacle to eliminating the waiting week. DOL now requires a one-week waiting period before applicants may receive extended U.I. benefits or states will lose the federal portion of funding for the benefits. (Extended benefits provide the long term unemployed with additional weeks of benefits during periods of high unemployment. Unfortunately, the program was altered in 1981 to make it more difficult for the federal benefits to be "triggered on" in a state.) Many states now are revising their laws to be in conformity with this DOL ruling regarding the waiting week. However, those states, which have lower jobless rates and which rarely tap the extended benefits program, are choosing to maintain their existing laws and allow for no waiting period before benefit payments begin.

If such a legislative change is politically impossible, employment advocates could consider doing what nine other states do -- compensating the claimants for the waiting week if their period of joblessness exceeds a specified number of weeks (usually this ranges from three to nine weeks.) In other words, if a person is unemployed for five weeks, he or she would get compensation for the first week of unemployment. Louisiana, Missouri, Minnesota, New Jersey, Pennsylvania, Ohio, and Texas presently have such measures.

d) Benefit Levels

Legislation to upgrade state benefit levels also might be considered. Present benefit levels are miserably low in many states, resulting in financial strain for claimants and their families. The UAW, for example, recommends that states set standards of not less than 60 percent of the claimant's average weekly wage, including fringe benefits. A higher percentage of wages should be replaced for lower income workers as well. States also should consider enacting dependency allowances in order to ensure fairness to larger households as is the case in Alaska, Connecticut, Illinois, Indiana, Iowa, Maine, Massachusetts, Michigan, Ohio, Pennsylvania, and Rhode Island. Lastly, the UAW suggests that a partial benefit formula be created which provides strong incentives to workers to accept part-time employment.

Another important reform could be to increase the number of weeks of compensation coverage. All states provide a ceiling on the total amount of benefits any claimant may receive during a benefit year. Most states have pegged this level at 26 weeks. (Some, however -- the District of Columbia, Massachusetts, Pennsylvania, Utah, Washington, and Wisconsin -- allow for more.)

e) Other Changes

Frequently, employers challenge the right of individuals to obtain their benefits. State laws can also be strengthened in this area. The UAW recommended in a report submitted to the National Commission on Unemployment Compensation in 1979 that a variety of changes in the system be made.

First, they suggest that state agencies should provide simple information booklets to all claimants. Employers should be required to post notices of unemployment insurance rights in prominent places and hearings should be held prior to a cut-off of benefits. Unions should be contacted to participate in such hearings.

Establishing A Short-Time Compensation Program

The unemployment insurance system can be used to mitigate the impact of layoffs by establishing a short-time compensation system. Under a California law, instead of laying off workers, businesses can cut back on payrolls during hard times by reducing the workweek and letting employees receive partial unemployment insurance benefits. This method of work sharing is called short-time compensation. California presently is the only state which runs such a program.

Similar legislation has been enacted in the last year in Arizona and is just getting underway. The state of New York has proposed a demonstration project. And legislation has been recently introduced in Kentucky, Maine, New Jersey, and Pennsylvania.

The California program, enacted in 1978 by State Senator Bill Greene's Senate Bill 1471, helps both employers and employees avoid some of the burdens of a layoff. For instance, if businesses can retain employees during a temporary slowdown, they can more quickly gear up when business conditions improve. Employers are then spared the expenses of recruiting, hiring, and training new workers. In turn, employees are spared the hardships of total unemployment, and may maintain their fringe benefits during this period. Likewise, businesses who must reduce their work forces permanently can use the program as a phased transition to a layoff. Affected employees, thus, can continue to work at reduced levels with an opportunity to find other jobs prior to the expected layoff.

California's program is voluntary. But, if there is a union in the plant, the union bargaining agent must agree to cooperate. As of March, 1980, about 600 California companies and 12,500 workers had participated in the program. The average duration of the program for a specific firm was about six weeks. Total monies received by employees was about 90 percent of full time earnings for participating workers.

Organized labor is interested in this program provided there are safeguards. The AFL-CIO Executive Council issued a statement on the issue on August 5, 1981. It states that "union reports on the California experience have been generally positive." It further urged that in states where short-time compensation is to be enacted that: (1) unions have veto power over participation; (2) at least two-thirds of each employee's lost pay be replaced for up to 40 percent of the workweek; (3) pension, insurance, or other fringe benefits be maintained; (4) adequate funding for the unemployment insurance fund to protect all the jobless be maintained; and (5) recently hired employees, such as minorities and women, be protected against employers manipulating this system for their own ends.

Using Unemployment Insurance To Assist Retraining

The unemployment insurance system could be altered so that it is more useful to jobless workers who wish to receive benefits while being retrained for new employment opportunities. To do this, activists would get states to change their definition of "job readiness." In many states the present system creates disinincentives to unemployed individuals to be retrained, since they must take "suitable" work when it is available.

Often this makes it difficult for workers to obtain new skills and to shift from labor surplus occupations to labor shortage ones.

The California state legislature has already reformed this aspect of their unemployment compensation system by enacting Senator Greene's Senate Bill 1115 in 1980. This act enabled workers to enroll in certified retraining programs and simultaneously receive unemployment insurance benefits.

Another idea, proposed by economist Roger Vaughan of the New York Office of Policy Development, suggests a demonstration project, to allow recipients of unemployment insurance to "borrow" future payments to finance education, training, or relocation. Anyone who finds a job before his or her eligibility expires would receive a cash grant of a share of the saved benefits. This could be used to amortize a part of the "loaned" expenses. Thus, an individual eligible for one year of unemployment insurance who graduated from a commercial technical school and found a job after six months would receive a grant equivalent to three months of unused unemployment insurance benefits to defray training costs.

The Employment and Training Subcommittee of the National Governors Association has suggested another model. West Germany, they point out, has an unemployment insurance system with two tiers -- one that provides additional income maintenance benefits to those workers who are in qualified educational and training programs, and another for those who are unemployed, and searching for jobs that provide basic unemployment insurance benefits. States, thus, could enact a law that would increase benefits for workers in certified retraining programs.

Each of these strategies may be attractive to state legislatures and governors concerned about job creation and labor productivity. Moreover, some measures, like a short-term compensation program, may be easier to enact than reforms in benefit levels, and may provide organizers with some clear and quick victories.

ASSISTING VICTIMS OF PLANT CLOSINGS

An economic dislocation -- the sudden loss of many jobs in a single area, whether from a plant closing or mass long-term layoff -- is a recurring source of social hardship which deprives America of the full use of her potentially productive citizens. Because of the closings at Youngstown Sheet and Tube, and in the Zenith television plants in Sioux City, for example, large groups of workers were forced to waste the skills and job experience that allowed them to make their unique contributions to the economy. Wasting these individual resources and disrupting our communities is clearly not sound public policy.

The major, but by no means, the only victims are the laid-off workers and their families. Massive job cuts often overwhelm local employment opportunities. States and municipalities suffer, as their tax base erodes and public spending rises to pay for the social costs of economic dislocation, which include rapid increases in juvenile delinquency, crime, divorce, mental illness, and despair.

Passage of federal legislation will be necessary to deal effectively with economic dislocation. The major provisions of such legislation would include the following: (1) substantial advance notice of plant closings and mass layoffs -- to allow workers to find suitable new employment, and to give federal and state economic adjustment programs the lead time necessary for effective action; (2) removal of tax incentives for runaway plants -- so the tax system does not encourage firms to close established plants in favor of opening new facilities elsewhere; (3) job creation and economic development programs for the affected communities -- to attract new industries and jobs for the dislocated workers and their communities; (4) assistance for positive adjustment for dislocated workers -- enriched and extended unemployment compensation and support for job search and relocation efforts; and (5) reemployment and retraining programs -- incentives for employers to hire and give on-the-job retraining for dislocated workers.

In the absence of federal action, there is a role for state governments. Although states do not have the power to control plant movements and shutdowns, they can help to cushion the blow and protect the unemployed during the process. First, they can pass state plant closings legislation, to require prenotification of plant shutdowns and provide for severance benefits and community assistance payments. Second, they can create an Economic Adjustment Team, which would require state agencies in employment and social services and industrial development to provide comprehensive assistance to the victims. Third, they can help workers hold onto their homes, when their incomes plummet during their involuntary unemployment. Fourth, they can aid individuals in meeting their medical bills by maintaining health insurance premiums. Finally, they can implement programs which would encourage worker/community buyouts of closing, but still viable, plants. Appropriate strategies may vary from state to state.

Enacting State Plant Closing Legislation

Prompted by coalitions of citizen action groups, labor unions, and progressive state and local officials, a number of state legislatures now have plant closing proposals: Delaware, New Jersey, Pennsylvania, New York, Rhode Island, Connecticut, Massachusetts, Ohio, New Hampshire, Maine, Michigan, Indiana, Illinois, Wisconsin, Montana, California, and Oregon. Most state bills require six months to two years advance notification of plant shutdowns and major layoffs, severance pay to the terminated workers, assistance payments to the affected community, and extended coverage of health benefits.

While passage of national legislation is absolutely necessary to deal with the problem of capital mobility and economic dislocation, there are two strong reasons for state action. First, there are some significant ways to address the problem at the state level. Second, given the present climate in the U.S. Congress, efforts to pass state plant closings legislation are needed to build pressure and precedents for national action.

In fact, Maine and Wisconsin have passed plant closing laws, and contrary to the predictions of opponents, these statutes have not discouraged business investment and economic growth. Moreover, Sweden, Canada, France, West Germany, and the United Kingdom require advance notification of layoffs. American corporations doing business in Europe have prospered in those countries and still invest aggressively. Furthermore, prenotification is the critical factor which can allow government and workers to prepare for layoffs and shutdowns and best utilize adjustment measures such as employment training services and income maintenance programs. (Legislation in this area would make a program like the California Economic Adjustment Team work far more equitably and efficiently.)

However, it will be quite difficult to enact these measures. A broad based coalition of labor, neighborhood groups, minority organizations, and churches must be mobilized to the conservative business opposition which would be aroused by a campaign to enact state plant closings legislation.

Creating An Economic Adjustment Team

Although it does not prevent closings, another promising strategy to address plant closings is the creation of a state-sponsored Economic Adjustment Team. Such a team could be required to assist in retraining workers, placing them in new jobs, modernizing older business facilities, and meeting workers' basic economic and health needs.

California began such a program after being hit by a wave of major plant closings. The Governor issued an executive order creating an Ad Hoc Task Force on Plant Closures involving the directors of a number of state agencies concerned with employment and economic development.

The Task Force, after examining the causes of recent shutdowns and relocations, found that policies could be used to both avert some closures and to ensure that shutdowns caused as little harm as possible to affected employees and communities. The Governor enacted an executive order which created an Economic Adjustment Team consisting of staff from three departments and which was charged with responding to closings and major layoffs. When the Employment Development Department learns that workers have been terminated by a plant closing or major layoff, a mobile employment placement office is created to counsel and test employees, conduct job search workshops, refer workers to training and education opportunities, contact employers and refer employees to existing job openings, and provide credit and mortgage counseling. Classes on obtaining unemployment insurance benefits are held and the use of California's short-time compensation program is explored.

In responding to specific closings and their attendant problems, employees have received transportation assistance for commuting to jobs in nearby cities and counties, local banks have provided free credit counseling, and the resources of employment service programs such as the California Worksite Education and Training Act, and local Private Industry Councils have been tapped. (See Chapter Three.) In the future, the Team will begin to explore the use of employee ownership as a technique to avert some shutdowns, as well as work closely with the Economic Development Department on obtaining financing and technical expertise for converting industrial facilities to new and more profitable uses.

In designing a campaign strategy, it is important to note that while this program has assisted victims of major plant closings, the absence of advance notification requirements which allow for more planning and the shortage of retraining monies in both the state CETA and CSWETA systems have hampered the state in truly taking the "sting" out of a plant closing.

It is also worth noting that the program has been politically popular. Businesses fear the passage of stronger plant closing legislation, and have, in most cases, been cooperative with the state government in specific "adjustment" situations. Therefore, advocates in other states might consider pushing for tougher plant closings legislation than this, but also using an Economic Adjustment Team bill as a compromise measure.

Assisting Worker Ownership

Full employment advocates also might consider encouraging state governments to play a larger role in assisting worker ownership in plant closings situations. Direct federal support, which has been an important resource for employee ownership, will decline under the Reagan Administration. But some state and local governments already are assuming the lead by enacting legislation to stimulate employee ownership and to assist potential victims of plant closings.

Maryland, for example, has passed four different laws providing financial and technical assistance to employee groups trying to establish worker-owned firms. And Michigan supports employee ownership through a state office which informs the public, the business community, and other government employees about the nature and advantages of employee ownership. Other states, including California, Ohio, Virginia, and Massachusetts, are beginning to consider legislation to promote employee ownership. Indeed, facilitating employee ownership as an alternative to closures permits an opportunity for state and local governments to retain jobs and avoid paying compensation to the jobless. The size and scope of state governments make them ideally suited to increase awareness and understanding of employee ownership and to creatively use limited resources to stimulate its growth.

Policies should be implemented to save viable firms and protect communities and workers from economic dislocation. These policies must faciltate the transfer of ownership of still viable enterprises.

Initiatives could include the following: (1) advance notice requirements to allow sufficient time to assess the viability of the firm, to design an ownership plan, and to locate appropriate financing; (2) stricter requirements for corporate financial disclosure to allow the purchaser to assess the financial conditions of the plant and to provide necessary information to financial institutions; (3) managerial expertise and technical assistance provided by public and quasi-public institutions set up for the explicit purpose of helping communities and workers threatened with plant closings; and (4) more active involvement by the public sector in offering financial assistance to communities and workers attempting to save viable firms. An alternative to direct public sector financing would be public policies which would encourage the private sector to become more involved in business retention efforts. Such measures could include tax incentives, loan guarantee programs, and credit insurance.

Addressing Housing Needs

Unemployment can have devastating consequences for the jobless and their families, often jeopardizing their ability to hold onto their homes. Employment activists should consider promoting policies to assist terminated workers in making mortgage payments. There are two good models being proposed in California that organizers should seriously consider.

Senate Bill 1110 was introduced in April 1980 for aiding employees of industrial plants who are terminated by plant closures. The state would counsel employees on family budgeting and on working out an affordable repayment schedule on their home mortgage. The government also would work with lending institutions to negotiate an acceptable and reasonable method of meeting the obligations of the mortgage or deed of trust during the employee's period of unemployment. Presently, the bill is locked up in committee and is strongly opposed by the savings and loan industry.

Another legislative proposal is Senate Bill 1111, which would aid veterans who are victims of plant closings by restructuring the state's home mortgage loan programs. It specifies the amount of the initial payment and amortization of the balance of the purchase price which the veteran must make to the state government. The bill permits the state lending agency, in certain cases, to postpone interest and principal payments.

These pieces of legislation may prove easier to pass than some of the other plant closings measures. Business interests could, in fact, derive some "good will" out of working with a program like Senate Bill 1110, and could be convinced to provide support.

Maintaining Health Insurance

Victims of plant closings and major layoffs not only lose their source of income, but also may lose their health care protection.

Employment organizations could assist workers in maintaining their health insurance through innovative public policy.

California Senate Bill 1112 is a proposal to provide health insurance benefits to unemployed and disabled individuals who are eligible for unemployment compensation payments. Workers could maintain coverage of the insurance plan of their last employer or could elect to receive benefits under the minimal coverage plan for state employees. The legislation also earmarks state monies which would finance the coverage.

MEETING LOW-INCOME NEEDS

Recent Reagan Administration cuts in national social and human services programs, the elimination of the Community Services Administration and the transfer of federal authority and program responsibility to the states through block grant programs make state initiatives to meet the needs of low-income people even more important than they have been in the past.

Two strategies are: (1) using state welfare programs to assist the jobless to get decent employment; and (2) helping the poor and unemployed to obtain free medical care through the Hill-Burton Act.

Establishing Temporary Employment Assistance Programs

Full employment organizations could devote some of their organizing energies to assisting those on welfare, who can and wish to work, to receive job training and be placed in productive employment. A good example of this type of program is New York's recently enacted Temporary Employment Assistance Program (TEAP).

On July 15, 1981 Governor Carey of New York signed into law the Temporary Employment Assistance Program, a project which will generate employment opportunities for general assistance recipients. The program allows public assistance grants to be paid directly over a six month period to private employers who hire and train eligible welfare recipients. The recipients will receive full compensation and fringe benefits equal to other employees at that level. It is hoped TEAP will thereby ease the often difficult transition from welfare to productive employment.

Under the bill, participating local social service districts will work out the job training agreements with private employers for home relief recipients who are eligible, needy persons who do not meet the categorical requirements of the federally-supported Aid to Families with Dependent Children (AFDC) program. The legislation appropriates $300,000 to cover program start-up administrative costs. Approximately 1000 home relief recipients will be enrolled in the program during the first year.

Using The Hill-Burton Act

Full employment advocates could help the jobless and poor obtain free or low-cost medical care through organizing around the federal Hill-Burton Act.

The Hospital Survey and Construction Act, enacted by Congress in 1946, gives hospitals and other health facilities money for construction and modernization. In return, the facilities which received funds agree to: (1) provide a reasonable volume of services to persons unable to pay, and (2) make their services available to all person residing in the facility's area. The Department of Health and Human Services (HHS) is responsible for administering this program.

The act, thus, requires free health care in area hospitals which receive monies from HHS. Hospitals cannot deny an individual admittance because of a policy which requires a large, up-front deposit. Furthermore, those facilities that provide specialities (i.e., cardiology, podiatry, etc.) to individuals with Blue Cross and Blue Shield must make sure that persons on Medicare receive specialist care too. Finally, all Hill-Burton hospitals must notify the public with signs which detail the types of free services the facility is providing, as well as when free care is available.

To receive such aid, a consumer must ask for these services. Furthermore, only hospital costs are covered, not private doctor's bills. Hill-Burton hospitals may stop assistance once they have given out a certain amount of free care for the year. Recipients income must be less than the Community Services Administration's income poverty line -- presently $4,310 for an individual, $8,450 for a family of four, and $11,210 for a household of six, etc. The facility must provide the consumer with a written statement which says either when one can get free services or why they have been denied.

In fact, Hill-Burton hospitals may deny an application for a number of reasons: (1) income is more than twice the CSA guidelines, (2) the hospital has already given out its required amount of free care, (3) the services requested or received are not covered under the hospital's "Allocation Plan", or (4) Medicare, Medicaid, or other insurance will cover the services requested or rendered.

Despite all these regulations, individuals frequently are denied care. Citizen organizations like the Philadelphia Unemployment Project have assisted low-income people and the unemployed to obtain hospital services. Local legal services also can assist a consumer in filing a complaint with a Department of Health and Human Services Regional Office.

Full employment organizations, wishing to assist the unemployed to meet their health care needs, should analyze this program closely, determining which hosipitals in the community receive Hill-Burton funds and evaluating their performance in complying with the Act.

SELECTED BIBLIOGRAPHY

Best, Fred and James Mattessich. Short Time Compensation and Work Sharing: A New Alternative to Layoffs. Washington, D.C.: Council of State Planning Agencies, 1980.

An incisive analysis of the nuts-and-bolts of short time compensation programs. Includes useful information on European and California's programs.

Bluestone, Barry, Bennett Harrison, and Lawrence Baker. Corporate Flight. Washington, D.C.: Conference on Alternative State and Local Policies, 1981.

Provides a thorough documentation and analysis of the problem of plant closings and the rising levels of joblessness and economic dislocations caused by unregulated capital movement.

Chupp, Virginia. "Changes in Unemployment Insurance Legislation During 1979." Monthly Labor Review. April, 1980, 36 - 42.

Useful survey of state unemployment insurance legislative changes.

Kelly, Ed. Industrial Exodus. Washington, D.C.: Conference on Alternative State and Local Policies, 1978.

Widely used introductory study outlining an action program on the issue of plant closings.

Kolter, John. Unemployment Compensation. Washington, D.C.: Congressional Quarterly, Editorial Research Reports, June 27, 1980.

Excellent overview of national and state unemployment compensation system.

National Employment Law Project. Legal Services Guide to Federal Unemployment Compensation Law and Issues. New York, New York: 1977.

Comprehensive description of national unemployment compensation statutes.

National Commission on Unemployment Compensation. Final Report. Washington, D.C.: Government Printing Office, 1980.

Includes final recommendations of Presidential Commission. Provides an excellent and detailed overview of entire unemployment compensation system.

State of California. A Review of the Shared Work Unemployment Compensation Program. Sacramento, California: Legislative Analyst, 1981.

Describes and analyzes the performance to date of the California Shared Work Unemployment Compensation program.

Teal, David. _Unemployment Insurance: What Does Partnership Really Mean?_ Washington, D.C.: National Governors Association, 1981.
A series of essays on unemployment insurance.

CHAPTER FOUR:

PROTECTING THE RIGHTS OF THE EMPLOYED

Increasing job opportunities for the unemployed is not the only goal of a full employment strategy. An equally important goal is fostering and protecting "good" jobs, those with decent wages and working conditions. Helping to turn "bad" jobs into "good" jobs is an important role for state and local governments.

States have a stake in upgrading "bad" jobs. Bad jobs impose heavy social costs on both the worker and on society. The low wages, bad working conditions, poor or non-existent fringe benefits, and limited chance for career improvement maintain people in dependence and poverty. Such people spend their time unproductively alternating between unemployment, under employment in low paying temporary jobs, periods on welfare, and enrollment in training and public service jobs programs. People who have "bad" jobs are very costly to society.

In addition, states or regions with more good jobs have a stake in translating "bad" jobs into "good" jobs in all parts of the country. Maintaining a region or state with low wages is a threat to every worker. Raising the quality of all jobs across the country is in everyone's interest.

State and local governments can improve the quality of jobs and protect the employed by expanding collective bargaining rights, by defeating right-to-work bills, by upgrading minimum wages, by protecting Davis-Bacon prevailing wage laws, by improving workers' compensation, and by passing worker and community right-to-know legislation. These measures will enhance the long-term employability of workers and generate more "good jobs." Wages will rise. The numbers of work accidents will decrease and the healthfulness of work environments will improve.

EMPOWERING WORKERS

Presently, employees have fewer rights on the job than employers. Many workers have little control over the pace and organization of work, health-and-safety conditions, wage determination, and job security. Likewise, employees who wish to "blow the whistle" on illegal actions in environmental or consumer matters have little powers to resist resist employer attempts at intimidation, discrimintation, or retribution for disclosing information. Improving collective bargaining laws and giving workers additional civil liberties protections are two important strategies to address these problems and increase the "say" that workers have at their jobs.

Protecting and Expanding Collective Bargaining Rights

Across the nation, collective bargaining rights are under attack. In Louisiana, the National Right to Work Committee and their supporters were able in 1976 to enact the first right-to-work law in any state since 1963. Since then, a major effort to pass a right-to-work initiative was defeated by Missouri voters in 1978 and a New Mexico bill, passed by the state legislature was vetoed by the governor.

Employment advocates should ally themselves with labor and its grassroots supporters to meet this coordinated attack on trade union rights. They should work at preventing the spread of "right-to-work" laws to other states, as well as seek to pass new measures that strenght-en union organizing and bargaining rights.

For example, even in the conservative years of 1980 and 1981, state legislatures passed a number of interesting pieces of union-oriented legislation. Michigan, Ohio, and Wisconsin prohibited the awarding of state contracts to persons or firms found to be in violation of the National Labor Relations Act. California joined this group of states in 1981, and passed a measure which prohibited the awarding of state contracts to contractors who violated a National Labor Relations Board order more than once in the preceding two years.

A new public employee collective bargaining law was passed in the Virgin Islands, strikes by non-essential public employees were legalized in Minnesota, and public employees in New Jersey were authorized to negotiate agency shop agreements. In 1981, local public employees in California also were allowed to establish agency shop agreements, and in Maine collective bargaining rights were extended to county employees. The employment, recruitment, or transportation of strikebreakers to replace employees where a strike or lock-out exists is prohibited now in Wisconsin.

Full employment activists also must understand the importance of union security contracts, which in the United States legally take one of the following three forms: union shop, maintenance of membership, agency shop. In a union shop, all workers hired by the employer must join the union -- at least to the extent of paying dues -- within a specified time after they are hired. Maintenance of membership agreements state that workers who are union members when the union-management agreement is signed, and non-members who join the union later, must remain members for the duration of the contract. An agency shop is where workers must either join the union, or, if they choose not, pay to the union the amount of dues paid by the union members. State "right-to-work" laws prohibit each of these arrangements.

Right-to-work laws are misleading and unfair. They have nothing to do with creating jobs or protecting basic freedoms. All they do is stop companies from negotiating contracts that require that, if a majority of its workers vote to join a union, all the firms' workers must pay their fair share of the cost of union representation. Since unions must represent all the workers in a workplace, both members and non-members should share the costs of representation. "Right-to-work" laws allow some workers to get the benefits of union membership (from higher wages to family health insurance) without sharing the costs of winning those benefits. And in fact, 74 percent of all Americans do not "think it's fair for people to receive benefits from an organization, such as a labor union, without paying any of the costs of getting those benefits," according to the Task Force on Labor Law Reform, based on a poll it conducted in 1977.

In addition, the National Labor Relations Act, Taft-Hartley, and the Landrum-Griffin Act all safeguard the rights of individual workers. Such rights range from the protection of workers who wish to initiate decertification and deauthorization efforts, to allowing individuals to refuse to contribute to the union's voluntary political fund.

Finally, either repealing section 14-b of the Taft-Hartley Act, which legalizes state passage of "right-to-work" laws, or overturning the existing statutes in Alabama, Arizona, Arkansas, Florida, Georgia, Iowa, Kansas, Louisiana, Mississippi, Nebraska, Nevada, North Carolina, North Dakota, South Carolina, South Dakota, Tennessee, Texas, Utah, Virginia, and Wyoming would help to equalize wages and working conditions between states, and make it more difficult for right-wing campaigns to use the business climate argument to play one state against another and roll back legislative gains made by labor and other progressive forces.

Increasing Workers' Civil Rights

Employment advocates should expand the "civil rights" of workers on the job. In Michigan, a comprehensive "whistleblowers" protection act was passed in the 1981 legislative session. This law prohibits reprisals against public or private sector employees who report, or attempt to report, any violation of state, local, or federal law, or who participate in an investigation, hearing, inquiry, or court action. An employer may not discharge, threaten, or otherwise discriminate against such an employee. The employee may bring a civil action for injunction or damages, or both, and the court may require reinstatement, back pay, and other relief. Five other states -- Connecticut, Illinois, Louisiana, Ohio, and Oregon -- also amended individual statutes in 1981 to protect from employer retaliation an employee who reports a violation of law or participates in an enforcement proceeding.

In 1982, some promising measures were also enacted expanding the rights of agricultural workers. A comprehensive law in Minnesota grants seasonal farmworkers important new protections. These workers must now be paid for a guaranteed number of hours; are to be provided written pay statements itemizing deductions from wages; and are to be informed, at the time of recruitment, of the minimum duration of employment, and of working conditions, wages, and housing provisions, if any. Similarly, in Oregon, a new amendment requires that migrant workers be furnished with the names and addresses of their employers, with notification of any labor dispute at the work site, and with statements of hours of work and rates of pay.

ESTABLISHING DECENT WAGES

Millions of American households earn too little money to adequately support themselves, and a substantial majority of those households remain in poverty despite the fact that the heads of households worked at some time during the year. For most of the poor in this society, poverty is caused not by their inability to find work, but despite the fact that they work repeatedly, and often steadily. Ending their poverty would require, therefore, both higher wages on the jobs they hold, and more employment opportunities. Full employment activists should commit themselves to campaigning for higher minimum wages and preserving union-based wage standards.

Raising and Enforcing State Minimum Wages

Progressives should work on ensuring that state minimum wage laws are upgraded periodically and enforced. Minimim wage rates were increased in 26 states in 1981. Eighteen jurisdictions now have a minimum rate for some or all occupations equal to or exceeding the $3.35-per-hour federal standard, that took effect January 1, 1981. Two more states will reach the $3.35 rate during 1982.

In other minimum wage action, North Carolina extended coverage to employers of three or more rather than four or more as before. And in Oregon, persons over age 65 were removed from a list of those for whom a subminimum hourly wage rate may be set.

During 1980, two interesting laws were passed for tougher enforcement of minimum wage laws. In Oregon, the prohibition on discharging, or discriminating against an employee who has made a wage claim, was expanded to protect those who have discussed such a wage claim with a lawyer or agency. And in New York the Labor Commissioner may now order the payment of a civil penalty up to 25 per cent of the total amount found to be due under violations of the minimum wage and wage payment laws and regulations.

Protecting State Davis-Bacon Acts

Employment activists should enlist in the battles to protect prevailing wage laws. In the 1981 state legislative sessions, many bills were introduced to weaken or repeal "little Davis-Bacon" acts, which set prevailing wage standards for construction work financed by state monies. Although bills were introduced in 14 states, only the Utah law was repealed, an action taken over the Governor's veto. All the other repeal efforts failed, including bills vetoed in Colorado and New Mexico. Courts in Michigan and Missouri upheld the constitutionality of the prevailing wage laws in those states.

More positively, in other prevailing wage developments, Rhode Island made wage-rate violators subject to an 18-month ban on bidding for, or being awarded a public contract. The labor department in Montana was given subpoena power to compel the production of payroll records, and the prevailing wage rate is to be included in bid specifications and contracts.

New Jersey extended coverage of its prevailing wage law to any construction by the New Jersey Building Authority. Oklahoma mandated use of federal Davis-Bacon rates and required payment of prevailing fringes. And in the state of Washington, wage rates must be posted on the job.

INCREASING WORKER HEALTH AND SAFETY

Many workers are exposed to treacherous hazards on the job, including the risk of fatal accidents or potentially fatal, occupationally-caused diseases. Full employment activists, who are concerned about preventing workers from getting caught in a vicious cycle of low incomes, periodic unemployment, and poor health, should seek to strengthen state workers' compensation programs, as well as to pass employee and community right-to-know legislation.

Strengthening Workers' Compensation

Employment advocates should get involved in workers' compensation campaigns. Currently, states' workers' compensation programs are generating intense controversy in many state legislatures. These already inadequate programs have been targeted by business and industry groups who argue that liberal state worker compensation laws are bad for the "business climate."

Workers' compensation programs were one of the major victories of progressive and labor coalitions in the early part of this century. Enacted by state governments, these programs provide cash payments to workers who suffer injury or disease resulting from their job. Money is provided to disabled workers for medical care, rehabilitation, and actual cash assistance for living expenses.

Existing compensation laws are a national disgrace. Worker benefits are too low, business premiums too high, and the waiting time to begin receiving benefits is too long. And many disease-related disabilities are not covered at all.

A typical worker who becomes permanently disabled due to an accident on the job is likely to receive only a small fraction of what s/he could expect to earn through future employment. And benefits are even lower for those suffering from occupationally caused diseases. In fact, only 10 per cent of the two million workers who are partially or severely disabled by work-induced illness receive any compensation of any kind.

Despite the inadequacy of most workers' compensation programs, some industry groups are actively working to make the programs even less effective. A Michigan business group, for example, claims the state's meager program is driving business out of the state at the expense of needed jobs. Other opponents blame these laws for the difficulty in attracting new industry.

While the current situation is grim, progressives and unions are trying to work with state legislators to strengthen workers' compensation programs. They are calling on the states to comply with recommendations made nine years ago by the National Commission on State Workmen's Compensation Laws. The recommendations include broader eligibility, improved benefits, and greater availability of medical care.

Some states have bucked the national trend and are improving their programs. Washington and Ohio have upgraded benefits for their citizens by eliminating private insurance carriers from their compensation program and substituting an exclusive state fund instead. Through Washington's exclusive state fund, eligible workers receive $1.05 in benefits for every dollar paid in premiums. This is possible thanks to the program's investment earnings which more than offset the entire expense of administering the program. The Washington approach contrasts sharply with states in which private insurers pocket $.48 of every premium dollar, leaving ill and injured workers only $.52 per dollar.

Ohio's program has wide public support, as shown in the last election in which voters rejected by a 4-1 margin an insurance business-sponsored proposition that would have allowed private insurance companies to compete with the state program to sell workers' compensation insurance. With the help of state AFL-CIO chapters, legislators in New York, Rhode Island, Michigan, and Illinois are working on similar bills to create exclusive state funds.

Activists who are in states where the opposition to exclusive state funds is very strong should consider taking other actions. They could push for the enactment of legislation to create non-exclusive state funds, which would compete with private insurance carriers in the workers' compensation business. Second, they could reform the workers' compensation rate making process so that private carriers do not earn excessive profits.

In addition to enacting an exclusive state compensation fund, states should also reduce procedural and legal delays which almost always work to the disadvantage of the employee. California legal fees, for example, average about 28 per cent of workers' compensation awards. State governments and labor's state chapters might follow the example of the Ohio AFL-CIO chapter, which sponsors a program to educate workers about their rights and responsibilities and instructs them in dealing successfully with the system.

State and local progressives, labor, and citizen groups should also urge Congress to enact strong federal standards for state workers' compensation programs. With the health and lives of so many at stake, federal action is needed to augment changes at the state level.

These important reforms will not be easy to enact. Private insurers along with many employers have a great deal invested in the status quo. But with growing numbers of occupational hazards to safety and health -- dangerous machinery, noise, radiation, and an array of toxic chemicals -- has come a growing concern among workers and a willingness to take action to establish safe and healthful working conditions.

Enacting State and Local Right-to-Know Legislation

Full employment activists should explore the possibility of working on "right-to-know" campaigns. Presently, workers possess little information about short- and long-term effects of chemicals they work with. Containers of chemicals are usually poorly labeled, and complete hazard information is rarely available.

During the last decade, the labor movement has been struggling for tough national standards that guarantee workers a right-to-know what they are working with and the hazards of exposure. Unions, in fact, won a major battle in 1980 when a regulation providing worker access to exposure and medical records was promulgated. However, in 1981, this regulation, along with an important proposal by OSHA to label containers more clearly and completely, were halted by the Reagan Administration.

Since the federal government is being prevented by the Reagan Administration from acting in this area, unions and their allies now are organizing to pass bills at the state and local levels to require disclosure of information about chemicals being used in the workplace. Such legislation has been passed in California, Connecticut, Maine, Michigan, New York, West Virginia, and Philadelphia. And, in close to another dozen states and cities, legislation is being drafted and considered.

Employment advocates should become familiar with these bills and work together to improve the quality of jobs, as well as to protect workers' long-term employment possibilities, by passing right-to-know legislation. The scope of these laws varies from place to place, both in the number of chemicals covered and type of information provided, and the role of the community in the regulatory process. The New York law, the Philadelphia law, and the New Jersey Bill, provide the broadest coverage both in terms of chemicals covered and the type of information that must be provided. For instance, the New York legislation added Article 48 to the state's public health statutes. This article broadly defines "toxic substance" as "which is listed in the latest printed edition of the National Institute for Occupational Safety and Health Registry of Toxic Effects of Chemical Substances or has yielded positive evidence of acute or chronic health hazards in human, animal or other biological testing." The 1980 law (Chapter 55) also designates certain powers and duties of the Commissioner of Public Health, including the right of entry into a workplace and an authorization to establish employee and public outreach programs regarding toxic substances in the workplace. Philadelphia Bill No. 270 amended Chapters 3-100, 3-200, and 3-300 of the city code, to guarantee the right-to-know to community members as well as workers. In New Jersey there are two separate proposed right-to-know bills which would cover both employees and citizens: Assembly No. 3309, "The Worker's Right to Know Act," and Assembly No. 3310, "The Community Right to Know Act."

SELECTED BIBLIOGRAPHY

Center to Protect Workers Rights. Little Davis-Bacon Acts: State of the States. Washington, D.C.: October 1979.

Describes attacks on state Davis-Bacon laws and how building trades have fought back. Surveys efforts in twenty-four states to repeal or weaken such laws.

Crawford, James. "The Dismantling of OSHA." Nation, September 13, 1981, 205 - 208.

Surveys the Reagan Administration attack on OSHA.

Department of Labor. State Compliance With the 19 Essential Recommenda-3ions of the National Commission on Workmen's Compensation Laws, 1372-1980. Washington, D.C.: Employment Standards Administration, January, 1981.

Excellent survey of state conformity with National Commission recommendations.

Department of Labor. State Workers' Compensation Laws. Washington, D.C.: Employment Standards Division, August, 1981.

Reviews state laws.

Fraser, Doug. Supplemental Position of the UAW to National Commission On Unemployment Insurance. Detroit: UAW, April, 1979.

Outlines UAW positions on unemployment insurance system. Details a comprehensive reform agenda.

Gallagher, Michael and Richard Kazis. The Real Subminimum Wage Program. Washington, D.C.: National Center for Jobs and Justice, 1981.

Critically analyzes debate over establishing a youth-oriented sub-minimum wage. Documents extent of noncompliance, need for stronger enforcement.

Hill, Norman. "The Double-Speak of Right-to-Work." American Federationist. October 1980.

Carefully examines state "right-to-work" laws and their impacts.

Hunter, Will. The New Right: A Growing Force in State Politics. Washington, D.C.: Conference on Alternative State and Local Policies. 1980.

Comprehensive report on "new right" activity, including right to work efforts and attacks on prevailing wage legislation.

Levitan, Sar and Richard Belous. More Than Subsistence: Minimum Wages for the Working Poor. Baltimore: Johns Hopkins University Press, 1979.

Excellent defense of minimum wage laws for reducing poverty and serving as work incentives.

National Commission on State Workmens' Compensation Laws. Final Report. Washington, D.C.: Government Printing Office, 1972.

Excellent overview of workers' compensation, includes excellent recommendations for reform.

Nelson, Richard. "State Labor Legislation Enacted in 1980." Monthly Labor Review. January, 1981, 1-14.

Surveys state legislative trends.

Nelson, Richard. "State Labor Legislation Enacted in 1981." Monthly Labor Review. January, 1982, 1-14.

Pollit, Daniel. "Union Security in America." American Federationist. October, 1973.

Critically examines arguments for union security contracts.

State of California. Community Right-to-Know: A Handbook on Toxic Substances Disclosure. Sacramento: Governor's Office, February, 1982.

Excellent overview of the issue. Includes sample legislation from a number of states and cities.

U.S. Congress. Senate Banking, Housing, and Urban Affairs Committee, Subcommittee on Economic Stabilization. Hearing on the Economic Impact of Payroll Taxes. 96th Congress, 2nd Session, Washington, D.C.: Government Printing Office, 1980.

Contains liberal and conservative testimony on the impact of unemployment insurance and social security taxes on job creation.

U.S. Congress. House Ways and Means Committee, Subcommittee on Oversight. Federal Provisions for Special Employee Income Protection Programs and the Unemployment Insurance program. 96th Congress, 2nd Session. Washington, D.C.: Government Printing Office, 1980.

Useful survey of national unemployment insurance programs, trade adjustment assistance, Redwoods program, etc.

SELECTED ORGANIZATIONAL RESOURCES

Employment advocates should contact AFL-CIO state and local Central Labor Councils, which are located in every state and in major cities. These councils should be an excellent source of information on employment programs and conditions, as well as a key source of technical expertise.

In order to gather information about both proposed and existing state employment programs, they should begin to work with state legislatures and state executive departments. Within the legislatures, senate and house committees on Business and Commerce and the staff departments of Bill Analysis and Legal Research, Bill Status, Public Information, and Research and Policy Analysis are the most relevant. The Council of State Governments in Lexington, Kentucky publishes an excellent yearly guide to these institutions. In addition, activists should communicate with state Departments of Economic Development, Labor, Manpower Development, Commerce, and others which have administrative responsibilities in the employment area. The following organizations are also excellent contacts:

AFL-CIO
815 16th St., N.W.
Washington, DC 20006
(202) 637-5000

Membership organization of private and public sector trade unions, researching national, state, and local employment programs.

California Public Investment Task Force
Governor's Office
107 So. Broadway, Rm.8020
Los Angeles, CA 90012
(213) 620-4362

Investigates new alternative investments for state pension funds in housing, small businesses and energy.

Center for Community Change
1000 Wisconsin Ave., N.W.
Washington, DC 20007
(202) 338-6310

Provides technical assistance to neighborhood and community organizations in rehabilitation and other housing and community development projects; also involved in disinvestment and neighborhood preservation activities.

Center for Community Economic Development
1320 19th St., N.W.
Washington, DC 20036
(202) 659-3986

Assists with energy-related demonstration and economic development projects. Publishes reports, case studies and other materials.

Center for Economic Studies
475 Kingsley Avenue
Palo Alto, CA 94301
(415) 328-1039

Researches the relationship between pension fund investments and job creation; investigates economic adjustment policies.

Center for Neighborhood Technology
570 West Randolph Street
Chicago, IL 60606
(312) 454-0126

Provides technical assistance in energy, urban agriculture, solar greenhouses, waste recycling and training; works in community-based economic development projects.

Community Economics, Inc.
6529 Telegraph Avenue
Oakland, CA 94609
(415) 653-6555

Provides technical and managerial assistance to neighborhood and community organizations working in rehabilitation and cooperative conversion activities; works on community-based economic development projects.

Conference on Alternative State and Local Policies
2000 Florida Ave., N.W.
Washington, DC 20009
(202) 387-6030

Network of local public officials, public policy analysts and community leaders. Focuses on state and local legislation in areas of economic development, agriculture, cooperative development, tax reform and energy.

Corporation for Enterprise Development
2420 K. St., N.W.
Washington, DC 20037
(202) 298-8771

Conducts policy research and disseminates information on targeted enterprise development programs.

Corporation for Public/Private Ventures
1726 Cherry Street
Philadelphia, Pennsylvania 19103
(215) 564-4815

Administers employment training and placement programs and researches national and state employment policies.

Council for Urban Economic Development
1730 K. St., N.W.
Washington, DC 20006
(202) 223-4735

Researches national, state, and local economic development policies.

Council of State Planning Agencies
Hall of the States
444 N. Capitol St., N.W.
Suite 291
Washington, DC 20001
(202) 624-5386

Membership organization of the policy and planning staff of the nation's governors. Provides technical assistance and performs policy research in economic development.

Environmental Action
1346 Connecticut Avenue
Suite 731
Washington, D.C. 20036
(202) 833-1845

Public interest lobbying organization. Works on environmental issues, including regulation of toxic substances and right-to-know legislation.

Environmentalists for Full Employmemt
1536 16th Street, N.W.
Washington, DC 20036
(202) 347-5590

Provides research and publications on the employment impact of national energy and environmental policies.

Full Employment Action Council
707 D Street, S.E.
Washington, DC 20003
(202) 546-6626

Research and advocacy organization of religious, trade union, civil rights, and other organizations committed to full employment.

Health Research Group
2000 P Street, N.W.
Washington, D.C. 20036
(202) 872-0320

Works on health policy issues, including occupational health and safety.

Human Environment Center
1302 18th St., N.W.
Washington, DC 20036
(202) 466-6040

Conducts research and advocacy projects regarding youth conservation work programs.

Human Resources Development Institute
815 16th St., N.W.
Room 405
Washington, DC 20006
(202) 638-3912

Functions as the employment and training arm of the AFL-CIO, encourages labor involvement in manpower programs, and operates 12 field offices.

Industrial Cooperative Association
2161 Massachusetts Avenue
Cambridge, MA 02140
(617) 547-4245

Provides technical assistance to beginning co-ops and worker-owned businesses. Performs some policy research in these areas.

Institute for Labor Education and Research
853 Broadway
New York, N.Y. 10003
(212) 674-3322

Organizing and educational group which works closely with unions, concerning employment, occupational health and safety, shop floor organizing, affirmative action, and discrimination.

Institute for Local Self-Reliance
1717 18th Street, N.W.
Washington, DC 20009
(202) 232-4108

Provides information and technical assistance to local groups on community-based housing and development projects.

Massachusetts Urban Reinvestment Action Group
3710 Washington Street
Boston, MA 02130

(617) 522-2077

Advocacy organization, specializing in urban reinvestment projects.

Minnesota Project
618 East 22nd Street
Minneapolis, MN 55404

(612) 870-8700

Research and technical assistance on alternative investments for public pension funds.

National Association of Neighborhoods
1612 20th Street, N.W.
Washington, DC 20009
(202) 332-7766

Works in support of neighborhood organizations by promoting local government decentralization and responsiveness to neighborhood-based development activities.

National Center for Appropriate Technology
P.O. Box 3838
Butte, MT 59701
(406) 494-4577

Offers technical assistance, scientific and technological research, small grants and information to primarily low-income groups working with appropriate technology and self-help projects in areas such as food, housing and energy.

National Center for Economic Alternatives
2000 P Street, N.W., Suite 200
Washington, DC 20036
(202) 833-3208

Researches progressive employment and anti-inflation policies.

National Center for Employee Ownership
4836 South 28th Street
Arlington, VA 22206
(703) 931-2757

Clearinghouse of conferences and literature on employee ownership. Publishes quarterly newsletter and counsels companies considering the creation of Employee Stock Ownership Plans.

National Conference of State Legislators
Hall of the States
444 No. Capitol Street
Washington, DC 20001
(202) 624-5400

Monitors state legislation.

National Congress for Community Economic Development
1029 Vermont Avenue, N.W.
Washington, DC 20005
(202) 659-8411

National membership organization of Community Development Corporations. Provides policy research, as well as monitoring relevant state and federal legislation.

National Council on Employment Policy
2000 K. St., N.W.
Suite 454
Washington, D.C. 20006
(202) 833-2532

Publishes reports on national employment training and placement programs.

National Council of Churches
Full Employment Committee, Washington Office
110 Maryland Ave., N.E.
Washington, DC 20006
(202) 544-2350

Employment research, advocacy and information dissemination organization.

National Economic Development and Law Center
2150 Shattuck Ave. Suite 300
Berkeley, CA 94704
(415) 548-2600

Provides legal support and technical services to community development corporations and offers legal services programs in the field of economic development.

National Employment Law Project
236 Massachusetts Avenue, N.E.
Suite 505
Washington, D.C. 20002
(202) 544-2185

Monitors national legislation for Legal Services Corporations on CETA, youth employment issues, labor policies, and employment discrimination.

National Governors Association
Hall of the States
444 N. Capitol Street
Washington, DC 20001
(202) 624-5300

Provides input into state-federal policy issues for state governors. Provides technical assistance to state governments, publicizing innovative policy approaches through publications.

National Rural Center
1828 L Street, N.W.
Washington, DC 20036
(202) 331-0258

Develops and advocates economic development alternatives relating to rural needs by conducting demonstration projects, using the results of existing research, evaluating federal programs and pursuing basic research.

National Training and Information Center
1123 West Washington Ave.
Chicago, IL 60607
(312) 243-3035

Provides training for community organizers focusing on neighborhood investment issues, especially bank regulatory practices.

National Urban Coalition
1201 Connecticut Avenue, N.W.
Suite 400 Washington, DC 20006
(202) 331-2400

Administer employment placement and training programs in 35 cities in the U.S.

Ohio Public Interest Campaign
340 Chester, 12th Building
Cleveland, Ohio 44114
(216) 861-5200

Researches and organizes around plant closings.

Peoples' Business Commission
1346 Connecticut Ave., N.W.
Washington, DC 20005
(202) 466-2823

Conducts public education program around issues of alternative investments of public pension funds.

Philadelphia Unemployment Project
1321 Arch Street
Room 506
Philadelphia, Pennsylvania 19107
(215) 564-3770

Organizes around employment issues including plant closings, unemployment insurance, and CETA.

Rural America, Inc.
1346 Connecticut Ave., N.W.
Washington, DC 20005
(202) 659-2800

Represents rural interests by providing information and technical assistance on rural economic and community development programs.

Wider Opportunities for Women
1511 K. Street, N.W.
Washington, D.C. 20005
(202) 638-3143

Promotes equal opportunity for women through model projects, advocacy, research, and training.

PUBLICATIONS

DIVESTING FROM SOUTH AFRICA: A PRUDENT APPROACH FOR PENSION FUNDS

This important new study answers the critical question: "How is portfolio performance affected by a divestment/exclusion strategy?". The authors prove through statistical analysis that a divestment program will not adversely affect either rate of return or risk. A critique of current anti-apartheid strategies is given, concluding that other methods have been ineffective compared to divestment. The book also contains a description of methods for combining divestment with constructive reinvestment in the local economy.
By Laurence Litvak, Julia Estrella and Kathleen McTigue (1981, 53 pp.) $5.95/$11.95 Institutions.
ISBN 0-89788-058-7

PLANT CLOSING: RESOURCES FOR PUBLIC OFFICIALS, TRADE UNIONISTS AND COMMUNITY LEADERS

What are the strategies used by trade union and citizen groups to control and restrict plant closings? This extremely useful resource manual describes the various organizing and legislative campaigns used in states such as Ohio, Pennsylvania, Illinois, and Massachusetts. Another important feature is a description of the strong laws which prevent sudden plant shutdowns in Europe.
Co-published with the Ohio Public Interest Campaign (1979, 85 pp.) $5.95/$11.95 Institutions.
ISBN 0-89788-012-9

PLANT CLOSINGS BRIEFING BOOK: ISSUES, POLITICS AND LEGISLATION

This valuable book examines the strengths and weaknesses of all legislation introduced in Congress and the states to control plant closings. Additionally, several chapters look at the underlying economic causes of plant closings, and a final chapter offers the best available bibliography of books, articles, and key organizations.
Edited by William Schweke (1980, 70 pp.) $5.95/$11.95 Institutions.
ISBN 0-89788-024-2

EMPLOYEE OWNERSHIP: ISSUES, RESOURCES AND LEGISLATION

An innovative free enterprise solution to such critical problems as plant closings, unemployment and worker dissatisfaction, employee ownership also has the distinction of being supported by both George McGovern and Ronald Reagan.
This definitive handbook on the subject includes a thorough description of how employee ownership works, emphasizing the two major forms, Employee Stock Ownership Plans (ESOPs) and worker cooperatives. The book answers concerns expressed by management and labor, details the social and economic benefits, describes federal assistance available, and perhaps most importantly, spells out a step-by-step program for state and local governments to encourage employee ownership.
By Corey Rosen of the National Center for Employee Ownership (1981, 75 pp.) $6.95/$13.95 Institutions.
ISBN 0-89788-052-8

MANDATING SOCIAL PRUDENCE: A HANDBOOK FOR PENSION INVESTMENT

What goes into creating a socially responsible pension plan? This handbook discusses the legal nuts and bolts of mandating social investments at each stage in the development of an investment plan. By making use of previously unpublished pension plan documents which mandate social prudence, the author provides the most complete picture ever published on the subject.
By Michael T. Leibig (1982, 100 pp.) $6.95/$13.95 Institutions.
ISBN 0-89788-065-X

THE STATE AND LOCAL TAX REVOLT

The State and Local Tax Revolt answers the question: what can be done to improve the efficiency and the equity of state and local taxes?

Chapters address such critical issues as: reforming assessment pratices - property tax classification - tenants and the property tax - protecting agricultural land - taxing urban speculation - wealth related disparities in school finance - user charges - economic impact of state and local business taxes.

The editors have compiled a broad range of narrative and statistical material, including hard-to-find articles, government reports, and special documents. These materials are logically ordered and tightly edited to help the reader fully understand the complex subject of state and local taxation.

This remarkably comprehensive reference book provides answers and in-depth explanations to such questions as:

- Do higher business taxes stunt economic growth?
- How can property tax administration be improved?
- How can farm and open land be protected by tax policy?
- Are circuit breakers or tax and spending limitations the best means of property tax relief?

Edited by Dean Tipps and Lee Webb (1981, 380 pp.) $9.95/$19.95 Institutions
ISBN 0-89788-010-2

WAYS & MEANS: REPORTING ON INNOVATIVE APPROACHES TO STATE AND LOCAL GOVERNMENT

If you want to keep up with the fast-breaking developments in state and local politics and programs, *Ways & Means* is for you. This bimonthly newsletter provides accurate and incisive news and information on what's happening at the state and local level in a broad range of issue areas.
Articles include news and analysis of local elections, organizing campaigns and legislative efforts; as well as useful resources, such as notices of upcoming conferences, new studies and reports and new organizations.
Six issues yearly, 12 pages. $10.00/$20.00 Institutions.

Please ship immediately the following titles:

Qty.	*Title*	*Price*

Pricing: "Institutional" prices should be used by business concerns and Federal agencies. **TOTAL** ______

☐Send complete publications catalog listing over 40 economic development, energy and agriculture policy titles.

Name ______

Organization ______

Street ______

City/State/Zip ______

Send order with payment to:
Conference Publications 2000 Florida Ave., NW
Room 400B Washington, D,C, 20009 (202) 387-6030